1000 BEST GOLF JOKES & STORIES

Sheila & Ron Stewart

1000 BEST GOLF JOKES & STORIES

Copyright © 2009
by Ron & Sheila Stewart

ISBN: 0-9717617-2-8

Published by
Acadia Scale Press

Printed in U.S.A.

Books by Sheila & Ron Stewart

**500 All Time Funniest Golf Jokes,
Stories & Fairway Wisdom**

**500 All Time Funniest Jokes
& Stories About Sex**

**500 All Time Funniest Jokes
& Stories About Gambling**

**500 More All Time Funniest Golf Jokes,
Stories & Fairway Wisdom**

**Another 500 All Time Funniest Golf Jokes,
Stories & Fairway Wisdom**

1000 Best Golf Jokes & Stories

Dogs & Clouds & Love & Life

The Professor Murders

The Sandstorm Connection

For everyone who enjoys sharing a game of golf, and sharing a laugh when all is not going as planned.

1000 BEST GOLF JOKES & STORIES

The difference between a bad day golfing and a good day golfing: A good sense of humor.

A golfer's bag contained fourteen clubs and a paint roller, because when he asked his wife if he could go golfing she informed him, "Not unless you can paint and golf at the same time."

My wife counts the strokes in her golf game in much the same way that she balances her bank book. If she forgets to enter a few small amounts here and there she doesn't worry about it.

"I need to work on lowering my golf score. Has anybody seen my pencil?"

The prettiest drive in my golf game this morning landed two feet from the pin on the seventh hole. It would have been even prettier if it hadn't been my second drive from the tee on the third hole.

"When do you decide that it's too cold to golf?" a golfer was asked.

"When I slice my ball into the lake," he replied. "And it bounces."

"What's the rough like on this course?" a golfer asked another golfer who was about to take his first drive of the day.

"Don't know," the golfer on the tee replied. "I haven't hit my ball yet."

What does a lush green golf course have in common with a golfer's description of his game?

A lot of fertilizer.

"So it's raining a little," a husband exclaimed. "You and I aren't bothered by a little rain, are we?"

"Why is he telling you not to be bothered by a little rain?" a visitor asked his wife.

"He's not talking to me," the wife replied. "He's talking to his golf bag."

I finally found a swing that I can repeat every time. Too bad it isn't a good swing.

I like to play with golfers who are better than I am, because it seems to pull up my game.

Of course golfers who are better than I am don't like to play with me, for the opposite reason.

Nobody is happier than a golfer with a good disposition. On the other hand, nobody is grumpier than a golfer with a bad disposition.

Two methods of determining the quality of a golfer's shot can be made by watching golf club acceleration and de-acceleration . . . as the club goes back into the bag.

"Do you pay a high price for golf?" a golfer was asked as he left the club house.

"I will today," the golfer replied. "I didn't tell my wife I was coming here."

My wife has started to golf with me, but I don't think she quite understands the concept. When I go golfing I take a golf bag and fourteen clubs. When she goes golfing she takes a golf bag, fourteen clubs, and three suitcases.

You're never too old to learn a new golf swing, and another new golf swing, and another new golf swing, and another new golf swing . . . .

"Do you ever pray while golfing?" a golfer was asked.

"Sure do," he answered.

"Does it help your game?" he was asked.

"Sure does," he replied. "I haven't hit anybody yet."

Why is it?

If we hit a golf ball into the rough, everybody can tell us what we did wrong. If we hit a golf ball straight down the fairway, nobody can tell us what we did right.

A golfer who had a dozen penalty strokes on a single hole decided that, technically speaking, she should be allowed to refer to them in the same manner she would refer to a carton of eggs. So she took a one.

A husband wanted to save money by teaching his wife how to play golf, until she persuaded him that lessons from a golf pro might be cheaper than half a house, his retirement account, stocks and bonds, and a divorce lawyer.

"When did you decide you were going to marry me?" a husband asked his wife.

"When you took me golfing," she said.

"Really?" he exclaimed.

"Yes," she replied. "I knew if we could make it through that, we could make it through a little thing like marriage."

The Pilgrims had landed on Plymouth Rock and were getting ready to explore inland.

"Too many trees to clear," said the Irishman.

"Too many rivers and lakes to cross," said the Welshman.

"The terrain is much too rough," said the Englishman.

"Good place for a golf course," said the Scotsman.

I very seldom make the same mistake twice in golf. But then I very seldom do anything twice in golf.

"My husband has named his golf clubs."

"Really? What has he named them?"

"Dirty, Rotten, Miserable, Low down, Water Seeking, Rough Loving . . . ."

"And which club has which name?"

"All of them."

You can always tell a person who has never played golf before. He's the one who's impressed by your game.

Two archaeologists were discussing their findings.

"During one of our searches," one of them said, "we uncovered a 5000 year old city. And adjacent to the city we found what we believe to be an ancient golf course."

"What makes you think it's a golf course?" the second archaeologist asked.

"Among other things," the first archaeologist answered, "we found a prehistoric five iron."

"And just how far into the earth did you have to dig to find this prehistoric five iron?" the second archaeologist inquired.

"We didn't have to dig at all," the first archaeologist replied. "It was wrapped around a tree."

Only on a golf course could eight people on ten acres be considered crowded.

A golfer was asked if he had ever had a bad day on the golf course.

"A bad day on the golf course," he replied, "is when I can't get a tee time."

First golfer: "I used to shoot golf in the nineties, until my wife said that I should get out and play more, and now my score is in the seventies."
Second golfer: "I wish I had a score like that."
Third golfer: "I wish I had a wife like that."

Every once in a while we need to remind ourselves that golf is just a game.

"Is your husband a good shot maker?" one wife asked another as a husband prepared to take his first drive of the day.

"My husband is a phenomenal shot maker," the second wife responded.

"Really," the first wife said. "How many phenomenal shots would you say he makes in an average game?"

"Oh," the second wife replied, "I would say at least a hundred."

The fastest way to ruin a good golf swing? Put a ball in front of it.

Golf courses sometimes make a request that golfers repair ball marks that are made from golf balls that land on the greens.

To which a member of a foursome responded, "Why? We didn't put them there."

Minister at funeral: "We gather here today to say a fond farewell to Henry McAllister."

Congregation: "Amen."

Minister: "As you all know, Henry was a golfer, and he passed away where he would have wanted, on the golf course he loved so much."

Congregation: "Amen."

Minister: "In fact, Henry's final act of love on this earth was to pull out his trusty driver and hit a towering drive more than three hundred yards straight down the middle of the fairway."

Congregation: "Amen."

Voice from rear of congregation: "I wonder where I could get one of those drivers."

Wife: "Wake up, I can't sleep, talk to me."

Husband: "What do you want to talk about?"

Wife: "I don't care. Anything."

Husband: "What if I tell you about my golf game today?"

Wife: "Zzzzzzzz . . . ."

"Do you ever worry that you might lose track of some of your strokes?" a golfer who had taken an abundance of shots on one hole asked another golfer.

"Not only do I not worry about it," the other golfer replied, "I count on it."

I have found one of the most important attributes to have when golfing is concentration. It helps me remember where my ball went.

Why is it, every time I'm first to tee off, someone in our foursome says, "Show us the way," but they never want to go where I go.

Sign in club house: Lost - five iron. Last seen leaving the fourteenth fairway.

First golfer: "See that dog over there? He barks every time a golf ball lands in the rough near their house."
Second golfer: "Why isn't he barking now?"
First golfer: "After a while he gets hoarse."

If you can't laugh at your own golf game, at least have the common decency not to laugh at others.

"Do you have any milk?" a golfer asked the young lady on the refreshment wagon.
"Sorry," she said. "We don't carry milk."
"Why did you ask her for milk?" another golfer inquired as he purchased a soft drink.
"Because that's what my wife sent me out for this morning," the golfer replied.

On the sixteenth hole a golfer was asked how many pars he had for the round.

"Let me see," he answered. "If I par this hole, and then I also par the seventeenth and the eighteenth . . . I'll have three."

"I see you're mentioned in the morning newspaper," a wife said to her husband. "It says you sliced your drive into a house along the fairway, then you went into the yard for your ball, then you got into a fight with the homeowner, and then the police came, took you away, and threw you into jail."

"And you said I'd never be recognized for my golf game."

Why do professional golfers find it easier than amateur golfers to add up their scores?

Because sixty-five is easier to add than a hundred and five.

A wife was watching professional golfers play in a tournament.

"Are the professionals' games similar to your husband's games?" she was asked.

"The professionals' games are certainly similar to my husband's *descriptions* of his games," she answered.

I played a really difficult golf course today. In one rough they had a map and a sign posted, "You Are Here."

I once shot a round of seventy-two. My score could have been lower, but we weren't rained out until the eleventh hole.

Four husbands had chores to do on Saturday morning, and to make the jobs go easier they decided to pool their resources. They would do the most difficult job first, then the next difficult, then the next difficult, until they had all four jobs completed.

First they had to decide which job would be the most difficult. The first husband had to paint the house. The second husband had to clean up the yard. The third husband had to remodel a bathroom. The fourth husband didn't have any chores, so he was going golfing. They decided to help the fourth golfer first, because after all, what's more difficult than golf.

The swing to a golfer is sort of like a personality on a blind date. When no one can think of anything good to say about your game, they usually resort to, "You have a nice swing."

"A golfer in our foursome has added twenty-five yards to his drives."

"Really? What did he change?"

"The way he describes his drives."

A retired man who spent most days on the golf course had a bumper sticker that read, *I'd Rather Be Working.*

"Why?" he was asked.

"Well," he said, "for forty years I worked and had a sticker that read, *I'd Rather Be Golfing.* For some reason I like this way better."

A wife, when informed by her husband that he was going out to shoot some golf, replied, "You can shoot all the golf you like. Just don't expect me to clean and cook it."

"I'm a little concerned about my husband," a wife said to the club pro. "Yesterday I caught him cussing his golf clubs because of his bad shots."

"That doesn't sound so unusual," the pro replied. "I've heard other people on the golf course cuss at their clubs when they hit a bad shot."

"But he wasn't on the golf course," the wife exclaimed. "He was out in the garage."

"I shot a hundred and twenty-two in my golf game this morning, and one of the other golfers said that since we were playing by winter rules, I could round my score down a little."

"I shot an eighty-five in my golf game this morning."

As a golfer prepared to take her second shot from deep in the rough, she noticed the bones of a human skeleton lying directly in front of her golf ball.

"What do you think we should do?" she asked another golfer.

"I don't know about you," the other golfer replied, "but I'd use a more lofted club."

A good way to stop one golfer from laughing at another golfer is to tell him it's his turn next.

Some first grade school students were asked what they would like to be when they grew up.

"A golfer," one student answered.

"Why a golfer?" the teacher asked.

"Because they have a lot of fun," the student replied, "they don't have to be very good, they don't have to study or practice unless they want to, and best of all, they get to keep their own scores."

"The worst confessions I have to listen to are from golfers," one priest said to another.

"Because they lie so much?" the other priest asked.

"It's not just that," the first priest replied. "Then they have to tell me how they lie."

A wife was attempting to put the car away in the garage when her foot slipped off the brake peddle. The car veered off the driveway, ripped through a hedge, swung through a neighbor's yard, and then came to rest in another neighbor's swimming pool.

"That reminds me," her husband said, "I have a tee time in the morning."

A golfer was showing some other golfers his score card.

"Wow, this is really good," one of them said.

"It should be good," a second golfer replied. "He's rewritten it five times."

"Have you noticed that no two swings are alike?" one golfer said to another.

"I have," the other golfer agreed. "We all seem to have a different swing."

"I'm talking about my own swing," the first golfer replied.

There are two kinds of golfers.

One golfer hits his ball into the rough and says, "I wonder how I did that?"

The other golfer hits his ball into the fairway and says, "I wonder how I did that?"

Hitting a good shot in golf is easy. Just think about where your ball is going to go, then do the opposite.

"What did you shoot today?" a golfer was asked.

"Ninety-six," he replied.

"Are you sure?" the other person asked with a touch of scepticism. "Everybody knows that a golfer's actual score and the score he puts on his score card are quite often different."

"They are?" the golfer exclaimed. "In that case, I shot a seventy-four."

Why is it? We can't hit a green, and yet if there is a tree between us and the green, we can hit the tree.

I once asked a golf pro why the ninth hole ended at the club house before golfers began the tenth hole. He said it was so we could restock our lost golf balls, or quit.

Two little boys were talking.

One says, "How come your parents named you Chipper?"

The other answers, "Because my father was golfing when my mother went into labor, and he happened to be using his chipper at the time."

"Wow," the first boy exclaimed. "What an interesting way to get your name, Chipper."

"If you think my name is interesting," Chipper replied, "wait until you meet my brothers and sisters, Putter, Driver, Sand Wedge, and Three Iron."

"Is it true," a person unfamiliar with the game inquired of a golfer, "that in the game of golf a low score is the sign of a good game?"

"Not with the golfers I play with," the golfer replied.

"How have your drives been today?" a golfer was asked.

"Not very good," he said.

"It says in my golf instruction book that to hit really good drives you should try getting angry at your ball," the other golfer suggested.

"So far my ball has been in two roughs, a lake and a sand trap," the first golfer replied. "I'm already angry at it."

TEN REASONS WHY YOU SHOULD BE ALLOWED TO KICK YOUR GOLF BALL OUT OF THE ROUGH

1 - You're saving your swing for the more important shots.

2 - You believe your shoe is straighter than your seven iron.

3 - You're getting in shape for fixing your lawn mower.

4 - Your wife doesn't allow you to swear.

5 - A kick doesn't count as a stroke.

6 - It's easier to line up the ball.

7 - It's easier to judge a kick's distance.

8 - It hurts too much when you kick your clubs, your bag, your cart, your . . . .

9 - It beats taking a mulligan.

10 - If it didn't want to be kicked, it shouldn't have gone in there.

Some days we play a really good round of golf, some days we play a really poor round of golf. A lot depends on which way the ball bounces.

Maybe it's the ball's fault.

"I shot a ninety-two today," one golfer said to another.

"You wouldn't be forgetting to add a few strokes, would you?" the other golfer said.

"If I were forgetting to add a few strokes," the first golfer replied, "you can bet I'd be shooting a lot lower than ninety-two."

"Does your husband believe that his golf game will eventually improve?" one wife asked another.

"Of course he does," the other wife replied. "In fact, he's believed it for more than twenty-five years."

A golfer borrowed a driver from the pro shop to try out for a round.

"Well, how was it?" the golf pro asked when he returned.

"It wasn't all that great," the golfer replied. "I could barely keep my ball in the fairway."

Another golfer who was standing nearby interrupted, "If he doesn't want it, I'll take it."

When asked what he considered to be the most important aspect in guaranteeing a good round of golf, a golfer answered, "Probably making the correct selection."

"In golf clubs?" he was asked.

"In playing partners," he replied.

A golfer was telling another golfer the best way to hit his ball out of some rough.

The golfer in the rough patiently nodded in agreement until the other golfer had finished with his advice and left. Then he leaned over and said to his ball, "You'd think we'd never been here before."

One golfer was watching another golfer who was fastening a suction cup to the end of his putter.

"What do you use that for?" he asked.

"I use it to get my ball out of the cup," the other golfer said. "It saves me bending down to retrieve it."

The first golfer thought it was a great idea. So he fastened a water ball retriever to the end of his driver.

One golfer hit so many golf balls into the rough, his caddy came with a search party.

First golfer: "I couldn't decide whether to use a hard seven iron or a soft six iron to reach the green on the last hole."

Second golfer: "What did you use?"

First golfer: "A hard seven iron, a soft six iron, two nine irons, three pitching wedges, and a chipper."

"I don't know if I should use a hard five iron or a hard four iron for this shot," one golfer said to another.

"Don't you mean a hard five iron, or a *soft* four iron?" the other golfer asked.

"No," the first golfer replied. "I mean a hard five iron or a hard four iron. No matter which club I use, it's going to be a hard shot."

A golf swing takes a second to execute, an hour to describe, and forever to learn - well, maybe a little longer . . . .

Why is it that greens always seem farther and smaller, and lakes closer and bigger?

"I canceled my tee time today because of the hurricane and the three inches of rain flooding the fairways."

"And you call yourself a golfer."

A golfer went to a golf pro to discuss problems he was having with his game.

"I'm just not a normal person when I golf," he complained. "I have a terrible temper, I throw my clubs, I kick my bag, I yell at the other golfers, I cuss and swear . . . ."

The golf pro replied, "That sounds normal."

After considerable laughter discussing the imperfections of their husbands, one wife asked another, "And where is your husband today?"

"Oh, he's off enjoying a round of golf," the second wife answered.

"How do you know he's enjoying it?" the first wife asked.

"Because he only left half an hour ago," the second wife replied. "He hasn't reached the first tee yet."

Young golfers see better than they aim. Old golfers aim better than they see. Middle-aged golfers aim and see about the same, which isn't saying much.

"Do you think this lake is too wide?" one golfer asked another.

"Not if you're aiming for it," the other golfer replied.

"My wife doesn't get too excited about golf. If her drives are reasonably accurate, she's happy. If her iron shots are reasonably accurate, she's happy. If her putting is reasonably accurate, she's happy. If her score is reasonably accurate, she's happy . . . ."

The real wonder of golf is that we can be so bad at it, and still enjoy it.

"Don't be so sensitive," one golfer said to another. "I wasn't criticizing your distance. All I said was, do you want me to go pick up your ball and set it back on the tee for you."

When a golfer announced that she had just purchased a new driver, the other women in her foursome asked if they could try it out. The first to use it had developed a slice, so she started her drive down the left side of the fairway.

"Bring it back, bring it back, bring it back," she coaxed as her ball drifted left, but instead of coming back to the fairway, the ball just kept going farther into the rough.

As she gloomily looked at the driver, as though it was somehow to blame for the poor shot, the woman who owned it said, "Don't feel bad, it doesn't listen to me either."

I once let my wife read the golf course layout map that is on the back of the score card. We began our game on the seventh hole.

A wife accused her husband of counting her strokes. "Don't be ridiculous," he replied. "I would never think about . . . that's five . . . counting your strokes."

I think my husband's hearing is going. I keep saying I shot par on the last hole, and he keeps saying, "Whaaat . . . ???!!!"

"Contrary to what your father says," a mother said to her children, "after God made man, he did not take a rib and make a golf club."

"Sometimes my husband fades the ball, and sometimes he draws the ball," one wife said to another as her husband teed off. "That was a draw. If he wanted to be in the other rough, he would have used his fade."

Golfer's friend: "I want you to know that I golfed with your husband almost every day for the past twenty years, and I was really sorry to hear that he died."
Golfer's wife: "He died????"

23

On a par five hole, if a bogey is six, why isn't a double bogey twelve?

Or going in the opposite direction, if four is a birdie, why isn't three a double birdie?

A retired man was asked if he had noticed many changes in his life since leaving the business world.

"Not too many," he replied. "The only difference I've noticed so far is that when I get up in the morning, instead of going to work, I go golfing."

A golfer who was preparing to hit a ball that was buried in deep rough was interrupted by another golfer.

"How do you know this is your ball?" the other golfer asked.

"If you could show me that this isn't my ball," the golfer in the rough replied, "I would be eternally grateful."

"I could never imagine myself taking up golf," a non-golfer said to a golfer. "To me it would be too much like a public flogging."

"Ah," the golfer replied. "I think I found your problem. First you have to imagine yourself enjoying the flogging."

"Are you the man who couldn't hit a fairway if you were standing on it?" a little boy asked a golfer who had arrived to pick up his father.

"Do you think your golf swing will change as you get older?" a golfer was asked.

"I certainly hope so," he replied.

As a wife prepared to hit her first drive of the day, her husband remarked from the edge of the tee box, "Don't forget to keep your weight on the inside of your right foot," as well as several other instructions to help her game.

When it was her husband's turn to hit his first drive, his wife stood beside the tee box and remarked, "Don't forget that we have yard work to be done," as well as several other chores that needed to be taken care of at home.

Then with a grin she turned to the others in the foursome and said, "I don't know enough about golf to annoy him with that."

"I've lost my swing," a golfer said to a golf instructor.

"Don't worry," the instructor answered. "We'll get it back."

"What makes you think I want it back," the golfer replied.

"When I told my wife about all the exercise I was getting on the golf course, she insisted on coming with me. That's her over there in the electric golf cart."

Two pigeons were flying over a golf course. They watched as one of the golfers hit a pathetic shot that missed the green by many yards.

"Even I'm a better shot than he is," one of the pigeons scoffed. "Watch this."

The pigeon circled and then did what pigeons like to do to whatever is unfortunate enough to be standing below them.

"Ha," the other pigeon laughed as he missed his target. "You missed."

"No, I didn't," the first pigeon exclaimed as he circled again. "That was my mulligan."

Golf is one of those games where you can have the best shot you ever made in your life, and the worst shot you ever made in your life, all on the same day . . . sometimes on the same hole.

"I wonder what it would be like to be married to the greatest golfer in the world," a golfer was asked.

"I don't know," he replied. "You'll have to ask my wife."

First wife: "Is it possible to hit a poor golf shot and not know what you did wrong?"
Second wife: "Not if your husband is with you."

Golfers were visiting the grave of a fellow golfer who had passed away. On the tombstone was engraved, "Herbert is shooting par in heaven now."

"I don't know what makes him think he can shoot par now," one of the golfers said. "He never could before."

"Not only that," the other golfer added. "I think he's on the wrong golf course."

A golfer was upset because he met another golfer who imagined his game to be as good as the first golfer imagined his game to be.

"Does your husband know a lot of different golf swings?" a wife was asked.

"Does he!" the wife replied. "He has swings he hasn't even used yet . . . there's one of them now."

A golfer who was all over the golf course was heard complaining, "I'd like to get my hands on the idiot responsible for the way these golf clubs hit the way they do."

"The problem with your golf ball landing in the rough," a golf instructor said to his students, "is that when you hit it, you sometimes get a flyer."

"What's a flyer?" a student asked.

"It's when your ball pops up in the air, takes off, and doesn't stop when it lands," the instructor informed him.

"That's the type of shot I've been looking for," the student replied.

"That's about the tenth time I've heard your husband tell that story about his golf game," a wife was reminded by another golfer. "Just how many more times do you think he intends to repeat it?"

"Not too many," the wife replied. "He almost has it down into the seventies."

If nobody knows the trouble you've seen, it's probably because they're in the other rough.

"I heard that your husband got into an altercation with a truck driver this morning."

"Yes. They had a disagreement over on the interstate."

"Was it before or after his golf game?"

"During."

The very best golf games often contain things they are not supposed to contain, such as good conversation and a lot of laughter.

A foursome of golfers asked a golf pro why the fairway on the first hole was so narrow, the rough was so high, the green was so small, and everything seemed to be surrounded by water and sand traps.

He said they made the first hole easy so golfers wouldn't become discouraged.

I asked my wife to see if she could get us a golf date during prime time. She did. We're teeing off at nine o'clock next Wednesday evening.

A golfer claimed to have hit a drive three hundred and fifty yards.

When asked if anyone had witnessed the drive, he had to admit they hadn't.

The next time he told the story, the drive was three hundred and seventy-five yards.

"My husband got angry after a shot and broke his five iron," a wife said to a golf pro in the pro shop. "Would you have a replacement?"

"I'm sorry," the pro answered. "We don't carry husbands."

"Two years ago when I began golfing, my husband offered to point out some of the faults in my game," one wife said to another.

"Did his suggestions help?" the other wife asked.

"I don't know," the first wife answered. "He hasn't finished yet."

"What were you doing up on the fairway a few minutes ago?" a golfer was asked.

"I was measuring its width to see what the odds were of hitting it," he replied.

"But you were also in the rough."

"I know. I was measuring the rough's width to see what the odds were of hitting it."

"And what were your results?"

"Well, the width of the fairway is forty yards, and the total width of the left rough plus the right rough is sixty yards, for a grand total of one hundred yards."

"So, what does that make your odds of hitting the fairway?"

"Forty percent."

Why is it . . . ? When I tee up my golf ball I try to remember everything I have to do. By the time I'm finished on the green I'm trying to forget everything I just did.

"Using this new golf swing I learned," one golfer said to another, "I made a hole in one on this hole, and then using the same golf swing, darned if I didn't come back the very next day and make another hole in one."

"That is just totally amazing," exclaimed the other golfer.

"That I got two holes in one?" the first golfer asked.

"No," the second golfer replied. "That you had two golf swings the same."

"It says in this book that golfers are among the most intelligent and imaginative of all sports people," a golfer informed his wife.

"I believe it," she replied.

"Really?" he exclaimed.

"Of course," she said. "You'd have to be to make up all those stories."

Another golfer said to me, "That was a really bad lie you had for your last shot out of the rough."

I didn't even know he was listening.

Golf is one of those games where everybody wants to tell us how to play, but nobody wants to take credit for it.

On the first hole a golfer took seven shots and gave himself a par. On the second hole he took eight shots and again gave himself a par. After watching this for most of the round, another golfer commented, "If it takes him that many shots to get a par, imagine how many it must take him to get a birdie."

A wife came home from a Saturday morning golf game with her own version of best ball.

"We decided today that if we didn't like our first shot, that we could take another shot," she said, "and then we got to choose which shot we liked the best, and we used the golf ball from that shot for our second shot."

"And which shot did you choose," her husband asked, "your first shot or your second shot?"

"My sixth shot," she replied.

"I've been working on a new swing," a golfer informed the others in his foursome, "and I'm really looking forward to trying it out."

He then teed up his ball and sliced it far into the rough.

"I'm not sure . . . ," another golfer who was observing offered, "but I think I've seen you use that swing before . . . ."

A wife purchased one of those scoring gadgets, where after each shot she moved a bead along a string to keep track of the strokes that she had taken.

At the completion of the first hole, her husband looked over toward her bag where the gadget hung and discovered she had moved a total of twelve beads.

"How come you moved so many?" he asked.

"I decided to keep your score too," she replied.

A golfer who was keeping score asked Charlie, a member of their foursome, how many strokes he had for the hole.

"Four," Charlie replied.

Then the score keeper turned to the other two members of the foursome and asked, "How many strokes did you have?"

"I counted eight," one of them said.

"I counted nine," the other one added.

"I didn't think you had that many strokes," the score keeper said.

"We didn't," one of the golfers replied. "We were counting Charlie's strokes."

"I learned a new golf swing. It doesn't work. I'd go back to my old swing, if I could remember it."

YOU MIGHT SUSPECT YOU'RE HAVING A BAD DAY ON THE GOLF COURSE WHEN . . .

- A little boy in the club house says to his mother, "Why is that golfer green?"

- Bowling is looking better and better.

- You hit a good shot, and the others in your foursome give you a standing ovation.

- You wish you were at home raking leaves.

- You describe your game afterwards, and it still stinks.

- You run out of golf clubs to blame.

- Your best drive all day was a ricochet off another golfer.

- The only green you hit is on the practice range.

- You step up to the tee, and people begin moving their cars from the parking lot.

- You feel really good about hitting a house beside the fairway, because at least you hit something.

- You begin to realize that perhaps you're not the greatest golfer in the whole world.

- For once you believe you got your money's worth.

A golf pro was watching a student who was not doing very well in a practice session. Her swings were slicing, hooking, catching only part of the ball, and sometimes even missing the ball completely.

After a moment the golf pro asked, "Which club are you using?"

With an optimistic smile the student looked up and exclaimed, "Do you think it could be the club . . . ????"

A golfer, who was having a bad game and getting a little desperate, prayed, "God, please let me hit just one fairway today."

After he completed his shot, another golfer exclaimed, "You did, you did hit a fairway. Now, stay right there while I go see which one."

A visitor noticed a strange man with a shovel and a rake in the back yard of a friend's house.

"What are you doing?" she asked.

"I'm not quite sure," the stranger replied. "I was playing a round of golf, and I was in a foursome with this lady, and she was having trouble with her swing, and she said that her husband usually helped her but he wasn't there today, so would I mind pretending I was her husband . . . and here I am."

35

I don't know why I'm always asking where the flag is on the green. Most of the time I can't hit the green.

"Do you think your husband is a good golfer or a poor golfer?" a wife was asked.

"A good golfer," she said.

"Why?" she was asked.

"Because," she replied, "when I think he's a poor golfer, he won't take me with him."

"Even after the lessons you gave me, other golfers are still laughing at my game," a golfer said to a golf pro. "What should I do?"

"I don't know," the pro replied, "but I'd appreciate you not mentioning the lessons I gave you."

Some of my longest drives are right after I say, "I might as well go ahead and hit my ball. I'll never get it as far as the group ahead."

Whoever said that practice makes perfect hasn't seen my golf game.

Yesterday a golfer in our foursome shot a game in the seventies. He did it the hard way. It isn't easy to hide eighteen strokes.

A husband was cussing his head off as he painted the house one Saturday morning.

"Why is he so angry?" a friend who was visiting asked.

"He's upset because he wanted to go golfing," the wife replied.

"For gosh sakes, why didn't you tell him to go?" the friend said.

"Because he'd cuss just as much there as he does here," the wife said. "The only difference is, he'd be enjoying himself."

The argument over whether men or women have the most intelligence can be decided at Christmas. He gives her a diamond necklace, she gives him a putter, and they both show the same excitement.

Today, I ruined one of the greatest golf games my husband ever played. I interrupted him while he was describing it to another golfer in the clubhouse.

A golfer's first drive hit a tree alongside the fairway. Teeing up another ball, he hit the very same tree.

"Hey, what do you know," he exclaimed, "I *can* repeat a swing twice in a row!"

After years of hundred dollar lessons, a golfer found the least expensive way to lower a score was still a two cent pencil.

A golfer was preparing to hit his ball back to the fairway from the rough with his nine iron.

"What's the matter?" another golfer in his foursome asked. "Isn't your shoe working today?"

A golf pro told me to play my own game. I don't want my own game. I want someone else's game.

Birds were sitting in a tree, watching a foursome of golfers.

"What seems to be the point of the game?" one bird asked.

"I'm not sure," another bird answered, "but I think they get points for hitting their ball into that long grass below us, or into that lake over there. Most of them are really good at it too, except every once in a while they miss and hit that short grass in the middle."

"Golfers on this course play by winter rules," one golfer informed another, "which allow us to move our ball to improve a lie."

"Really?" the second golfer replied. "And when do the winter rules end?"

"The preceding season's winter rules generally run until sometime in July," the first golfer said.

"Why July?" the other golfer asked.

"Because," the first golfer answered, "that's when next season's winter rules go into effect."

Two golfers were examining the score card of their playing partner, Jim.

"I wish I could golf this well," one of the golfers said.

"Even Jim wishes he could golf this well," the other golfer answered.

One way to learn the golf swing is to have another golfer, who says he knows more about the game than we do, watch our swing and offer suggestions for improvement. This will be just about any golfer we will ever meet.

"What was your score?" one golfer asked another at the completion of a round.

"I didn't keep score," the other golfer replied.

"Why not?" the first golfer asked.

"Because today was just a practice round."

"How come?"

"Because my wife said she didn't want me to golf."

"Then why are you here?"

"She didn't say I couldn't practice."

Calling yourself a golfer doesn't mean much to most people. Another golfer calling you a golfer, now that could mean something.

"My husband and his friends are reliving the greatest golf game they ever played," one wife informed another.

"Really," the other wife said. "When did they play it?"

"If they don't get rained out," the first wife replied, "next Saturday."

"What should I do if my golf ball is in an unplayable lie?" a beginning golfer asked an experienced golfer.

"Move your ball two club lengths, take a drop, and hit it from there," the experienced golfer responded.

A while later the two golfers met again.

"Well," the experienced golfer asked, "was your ball in a better lie when you took the two club lengths and a drop?"

"No," the beginner replied. "It was still in the lake."

"We enjoyed a really good round of golf today. We were rained out and spent the afternoon watching it on TV in the clubhouse."

"What's the difference between a happy golfer and a miserable golfer?"

"About twenty strokes."

"Are many of your players excellent golfers?" a prospective member asked a club pro.

"They are all excellent golfers," the pro replied.

"Really?" the prospective member said. "How would a person know that?"

"Easy," the pro responded. "Just ask them."

"The thing I have the most difficulty with in golf is hitting that stupid little ball. The most frustrating thing is getting that stupid little ball into that stupid little hole. I'd go back to bowling if I didn't have to carry that stupid big ball around."

The first golfer to hit his drive off the tee didn't see where his ball went.

"Was it a good shot?" he asked the others in his foursome.

"No," another golfer replied.

"Did it land in the lake?"

"No."

"Did it land in somebody's yard?"

"No."

"Did it go out of bounds?"

"No."

"Will I be able to find it?"

"Maybe . . . ."

"Then it was a good shot."

A patient went to his psychiatrist.

"I think I'm a bowler," he said.

"Why a bowler?" the psychiatrist asked. "Last week you thought you were a golfer."

"At what I pay you, I can't afford to golf," the patient replied.

Husband: "On the first hole I shot a par."
Wife: "Yawn . . . ."
Husband: "On the second hole I shot a birdie."
Wife: "Yawn . . . ."
Husband: "On the third hole I shot another par."
Wife: "Yawn . . . ."
Husband: "On the fourth hole I hit a ball into a lake and fell in trying to retrieve it."
Wife: "That hole I'd like to hear about."

"I use the same technique to remember the accuracy of my golf score that I use to remember people. What was your name again?"

You can have a lot of laughs discussing a golf game, especially when it's someone else's golf game.

"What qualities do you like to see in golfers you play with?" a golfer was asked.

"Let's see," he replied. "I suppose patience, good humor, understanding, interesting to talk to, friendly, being on time, keeping up to the group ahead . . . ."

"What about skill, drive, competitiveness, ability, desire to win . . . ?"

"Oh, I'm sorry. I thought you said, that I like to play with."

Two golfers met on the first tee.

"How come you're golfing on a Wednesday?" asked one.

"My company went on strike," said the other.

"I'm sorry to hear that," said the first. "Do you think the strike will last long?"

"I sure hope so," answered the striker.

"I let my wife use my driver in her golf game this morning. She lost her balance and fell into a lake during her back swing."

"I'll bet you were worried."

"No. Fortunately, it was an old club."

"I think your swing could be improving," a golf pro said to a student. "Even your slices are looking better today."

A golfer was searching for a lost ball.

"What kind is it?" another golfer who had stopped to help asked.

Sheepishly, the golfer who had lost her ball replied, "I was worried that my drive might go into the lake, so I used a range ball. It's yellow, with a blue stripe around it."

"One good thing," the other golfer replied, "I don't think we'll have to worry about someone else hitting it by mistake."

"Do you think I should worry about being hit by a golf ball?" A first time golfer asked an old timer.

The old timer laughed. "Do you see that green down there?"

"Yes," the student said.

"Well," the old timer replied, "if we can't hit that, what makes you think we can hit you?"

In golf, we can always recover from a bad first drive. It might take us four or five shots to recover, but we can always recover.

"One thing about rain, it separates the golfers from the non golfers. Want to go bowling?"

"I consider myself to be better than the average player," a golfer announced to the club pro.

"You realize that's not saying a lot," the pro replied.

"Do you and your husband get along since you took up golf?" a wife was asked.

"We get along very well," she answered.

"How do you manage?" she was asked.

"Easy," she said. "He golfs on Tuesdays, and I golf on Thursdays."

45

THE PUTT

He lined the ball up with his eye,
A simple putt to make,
One easy stroke into the cup,
Was all that it would take.

With confidence his putter moved,
The ball rolled straight and true,
It glided o'er the grassy green,
As to the hole it flew.

He knew not how it missed the cup,
Perhaps a blade of grass,
Had caused the ball to change its course,
And go on speeding past.

His second putt was lined up now,
Toward the cup it rolled,
He saw it take a solid line,
He knew he had it holed.

It must have been a gust of wind,
Or mark from someone's shoe,
Or dip or break or someone coughed,
That sent the ball askew.

He watched his third putt long and hard,
He studied all the breaks,
He squeezed his putter tight until
His hands began to ache.

The ball broke left, then right, then left,
Then ringed the orifice,
It didn't matter anymore,
He knew the putt would miss.

His fourth putt didn't take as long,
No worry or mistake,
He drove the golf ball off the green,
Into a distant lake.

****

A golfer named Shamus McDuff,
Bragged that golfing's not tough.
His swings were all strong
And his drives were all long,
But he hit every ball in the rough.

A golfer they called Dead Eye Dan,
Always knew where his golf ball would land.
His drives all took flight
To the left or the right,
Or the lake or the rough or the sand.

Some wives were asked why they took up golf.

"Exercise," one said.

"Fun," another answered.

"It will give me an opportunity to visit my husband," a third responded.

A husband learned he might be golfing a little too much when he informed his wife, "If anything should ever happen to me, I won't mind if you start dating and get married again. You can even let your new husband use my golf clubs."

"Oh, I could never do that," she answered.

"Why not?" he asked.

"He doesn't like your golf clubs," she replied.

"My golf score is lower than the score of any man here," the owner of a company bragged.

"It's not lower than mine," interrupted an employee, excuse me, an ex-employee.

"Who is the best golfer in your husband's foursome?" a wife was asked.

"My husband says that he is," she responded.

"And who does he say is the worst?" she was asked.

"They don't have a worst," she replied. "According to them, they're all the best."

A golfer in our foursome lost his number three golf club in his game this morning. He can't remember where he threw it.

A golfer was asked what the difference was between shooting a low score and shooting a high score.

"Eye witnesses," he answered.

The young golfer didn't hit a bad shot. It was in the middle of the fairway, but it had gone only a hundred and fifty yards. She watched as one by one the three men who completed the foursome stepped up and confidently drove their golf balls twice as far. She was feeling rather poorly about her game until another golfer reassured her.

"As I see it," he said, "there's only one basic difference between your game and their game."

"What is that?" she asked.

He gestured toward the three men who were scattering into the rough to search for their long drives. "You know where your ball is."

"They say that people golf to relax," one golf pro said to another.

"You could have fooled me," the other golf pro replied.

We should never display arrogance or a condescending attitude when a fellow golfer hits a ball into a lake.

Instead, we should offer comments that might encourage the other golfer, such as, "Good shot. Could you show me how you did that? Was your ball dirty? What club are you going to use for your next shot? I have a row boat at home if you need it . . . ."

Golf looks really easy on paper. If you don't believe me, just read a few score cards.

"What did your wife say when you informed her you were golfing Saturday morning?" one golfer asked another.

"She said she was really sorry I had to work again this weekend," the other golfer replied.

The quality of a golf game can change over a period of time. Some of the biggest changes appear to take place between the eighteenth green and the club house.

After five years of golf, I don't look at my game in exactly the same way I used to. For one thing, I occasionally get to look at it in the fairway.

"I noticed that your husband isn't swearing in his golf game today," one wife said to another.

"That's because I helped him get it out of his system before we came to the course," the other wife replied.

"Really," the first wife said. "How did you do that?"

"I had him instal a new water faucet in the kitchen sink."

On any given day, fifty percent of golfers on a golf course are enjoying a really good game, and fifty percent aren't enjoying it quite so much.

On any other given day, it could be the other way around.

I wondered why I was still slicing my drives after taking lessons, so I mentioned it to my golf instructor.

He said, "You know, I've been having a similar problem myself."

Golfers were attempting to straighten out their drives on the practice range.

"They say we learn from our mistakes," said one.

"If that's true," the other replied, "you would think we'd be a lot better by now."

"I heard that the owners are going to reduce the length of the golf course," one golfer said to another.

"Really?" exclaimed the other golfer. "Did they decide the length was too long for regular players?"

"No," replied the first golfer. "They decided to sell a hundred and fifty yards of the fourth fairway to a shopping mall."

One nice thing about rain - it speeds up the game.

"I might as well become a *@#$%*&%*$# forest ranger or a *@#$%*&$%*# sailor," a husband muttered as he arrived home.

"Does this mean your husband is thinking about changing jobs?" a visitor asked.

"No," the wife replied. "It means he's been golfing, and his drives have been going into the rough and the water again."

A man attempted to pay for his tee time with some currency the clerk didn't recognize.

"Are you asking me to pretend this is money?" the clerk asked.

"I don't see why not," the visitor replied. "You're asking me to pretend I'm a golfer."

My short game really looked good today. Unfortunately, I was playing most of it off the tee.

For forty days and forty nights, as the seas heaved and swirled, rains poured down upon him, and thunder and lightning crashed and lit up the sky, Noah drifted in the Ark with no sight of land.

He searched and searched to no avail, then just as he was about to give up all hope, a voice came back to him from beyond the bow of the mighty ship.

"Do you mind if we play through?"

A husband left his golf clubs leaning against the trunk of the car while he went into the house to answer the telephone. By the time he came out he had forgotten he left them there. Not thinking, he got into the car, started it up, and backed over them.

Later, as his wife and a neighbor examined the mangled clubs, his wife explained. "My husband did that to them after his last golf game."

Golfers are very positive people. No matter how bad their game is, they still think they're better than anybody else.

First wife: "My husband says they're going to pay someone to caddie for them today in their golf game."
Second wife: "Amazing! The next thing you know, they'll be hiring someone to carry their golf clubs."

Another golfer wanted to bet twenty-five cents on a game. I didn't take him up on it. I get nervous when I gamble.

"I'm a little concerned about where my ball might have landed after what that home owner said to me," one golfer confided to another as he looked over a fence to see where his errant drive had gone.
"Oh?" the other golfer replied. "What did he say?"
"You have the right to remain silent . . . ."

"There we were," a golfer said. "My ball was on the green and my playing partner's ball was in the water."
"Wait a minute," the other golfer interrupted. "That's not the way it was at all. My ball was on the green and your ball was in the water."
"Who's telling this story anyway?" the first golfer replied.

"Who taught your wife how to golf?" a husband was asked.

"Oh, it just happened," he replied. "We don't blame anybody."

"You'll never get a hole in one by hitting your golf ball into the lake," one golfer reminded another.

"So that's what I've been doing wrong," the other golfer replied.

"How many strokes did your wife record on that hole?" a husband was asked.

"About two thirds of them," he replied.

A golfer went to a golf pro for some refresher lessons.

"What type of problems are you having?" the golf pro asked.

"Nothing really serious," the golfer answered. "Just some little things, like my swing and my accuracy . . . ."

"What do you think about me making a two hundred yard drive across this lake?" one golfer asked another.

"That depends," the other golfer replied. "Did you just do it or are you about to try it?"

"I hit a drive today that traveled at least four hundred yards," one golfer said to another.

"Wow!" the other golfer exclaimed. "What did you do that was different?"

"Nothing really," the first golfer replied. "Once my ball hit the parking lot, it just seemed to take off . . . ."

Golfers don't like to take the blame when they hit a bad shot. They prefer to place the blame where it really belongs.

"Stupid place to put a house . . . !"

"Hardest thing I've ever had to do in my whole life," a wife complained after returning home from her first golf lesson. "And next week it's going to get even worse."

"How come?" her husband asked.

"Next week," she exclaimed, "they're going to give us a golf ball to hit."

Newcomer: "I gave up my last sport to take up golfing, because I heard that golf was less frustrating."

Golfer: "What was your last sport?"

Newcomer: "Bowling."

Golfer: "I think you might be going in the wrong direction."

I like the off season.

I telephoned the golf course and asked what time I could tee off. They said, what time can you be here?

AND THIS IS MY HUSBAND. HE'S TEACHING ME HOW TO GOLF.

My golf game is like the seasons. It takes all summer to get it going. Then fall comes and it dies. It rots all winter until spring, then I begin again. Then fall comes . . . .

Many a golf ball has gone into the left rough because we adjusted our swing to keep it from going into the right rough.

"My wife has finally learned to golf like a man," one husband said to another.

"That's great," the other husband exclaimed. "Is that her up on the green, getting ready to putt?"

"No," the first husband replied. "That's her over at the lake, getting her clubs out."

Our foursome has come up with a new incentive to lower our scores. We're trying to shoot the cost of a tee time.

"The most difficult thing I have in the game of golf," one golfer said to another, "is finding my golf ball when it goes into the rough."

"What about keeping your golf ball out of the rough?" the other golfer asked.

"O.K., two things."

"I'm not going to take golf lessons any more," one woman said to another. "I don't see why I should have to pay a golf instructor to tell me everything I'm doing wrong, when every man I ever golf with does it for nothing."

The swing is the most honest part of a golfer's game. We would like to lie about it, but we can't. There are too many other golfers watching.

"There's a fellow in this club house who improves our golf games every time we talk to him," an old timer said to a beginner.

"Wow!" the beginner exclaimed. "Do you think he could improve my game?"

"I'm sure he could," the old timer replied. "In fact, I guarantee it. Just a moment and I'll get him for you. Oh waiter, another round please."

One golfer is descended from Columbus. He wanted his golf ball to go east, and it sailed west.

"They say a picture is worth a thousand words," one golfer said to another as a ball sailed far into the rough.

"Personally," the golfer who had hit the wayward shot replied, "sometimes I prefer the thousand words."

A visitor, admiring a set of golf clubs, asked a golfer, "Have you ever considered getting rid of them?"

"Yes," the golfer answered. "After just about every shot."

The nice part about golf is, no matter how much a course aggravates us, we can always find another course that will aggravate us even more.

A football team was practicing in a field of mud. Rain was pouring down and they were soaked through to the skin. At last the coach saw the futility of trying to play in such poor conditions and called the practice off.

As they stood in the locker room, one of the players turned to another and asked what he was going to do for the rest of the day.

"Go golfing," the other player replied.

"My husband said he was going to take his golf game apart and put it back together," one wife said to another.

"How did he make out?" the other wife asked.

"Well," the first wife replied, "he got it apart all right . . . ."

Skills necessary to play great golf:

Drive your ball to the middle of the fairway, pitch to the center of the green, and then putt in for a birdie. The greatest skill of all is being able to convince other golfers that you actually did that.

I gave up golf because my game wasn't compatible with the fairways. The fairways were seventy-five yards wide and my game was a hundred and fifty yards wide.

"How come you're golfing today?" one golfer asked another. "This isn't your usual tee time."

"Oh, I upset my wife and she threw me out of the house," the other golfer replied.

"Have you thought about how you're going to get her to forgive you?" the second golfer asked.

"Not yet," the first golfer replied. "I've been too busy thinking about how I'm going to get her to throw me out next week."

A golfer returned a new set of golf clubs to the store and informed the clerk that they didn't seem to have any consistency. The clerk took the clubs to the repair shop to examine them. In a few minutes he returned and said, "I'm sorry, but I just couldn't find anything wrong with them."

"Hmm," the golfer exclaimed. "I wonder what else it could be."

An old timer and a beginner were talking.

"Which is more important in the game of golf," the beginner asked, "skill or luck."

"Skill, of course," the old timer answered.

"So once I've learned the skills, I should be able to hit any fairway or green on the golf course," the beginner said.

"If you're lucky," the old timer replied.

"I think my husband would make a great golf instructor, because he's so good at conveying his game to others. Just yesterday he was on the practice range, and the golfer next to him was showing him how straight he could hit the ball, and my husband was showing the other golfer how much he could slice the ball, and within no time at all my husband had the other golfer slicing his ball."

A golfer was asked, "Who would you prefer to play with? An amateur or a professional?"

"It depends," he replied. "Which one can finish eighteen holes in regulation?"

There is an old expression that goes, "If it walks like a duck and quacks like a duck, there's a good possibility it's a duck."

This expression should never be used to identify a golfer.

How do you know you are just about to finish the last hole: Your game improves.

There is a very fine line between a good golf shot and a poor golf shot. The line often runs along the top of a slope, just before it drops into a lake.

HOW TO TELL A DUFFER FROM AN EXPERIENCED GOLFER

A duffer is playing his first game today. An experienced golfer has been playing since yesterday.

A duffer is an optimistic golfer on the first tee. An experienced golfer is a duffer on the second tee, minus the optimism.

A duffer telephones the golf course and asks if he can get a tee time for eight o'clock Saturday morning. An experienced golfer telephones the golf course and asks if he can get a tee time.

A duffer wants to know where the fairways and greens are. An experienced golfer wants to know where the sand traps and lakes are.

A duffer is inconsistent. An experienced golfer is also inconsistent, but at a higher level.

If you see a golfer step up to a ball and just hit it, you know he's experienced. If you see a golfer step up to a ball and spend two minutes lining it up like he actually knows where it's going, you can be reasonably sure he's a duffer.

A golfer sliced her drive onto some airport property that was adjacent to the golf course. Without realizing where she was, she hopped over a fence and began searching for her ball. It wasn't long until a security guard drove up with sirens blaring and lights flashing.

"Lady," he screamed. "Do you realize where you are?"

She shrugged.

He continued sarcastically, "You didn't happen to see any airplanes around here, did you?"

She looked around. "There's one over there," she said, then added, "Now that we've found your airplane, do you think you could help me look for my golf ball?"

Friends are people who have played golf with us, and still like us.

I have a fairly good golf game, except for two areas. The front nine and the back nine.

When I aim for the green I hit the rough, when I aim for the fairway I hit the rough, when I aim for the rough I still hit the rough. You would think if I aimed for the rough I would hit something else.

An inexperienced golfer worries about hitting his golf ball into water, and consequently that's where it goes.

An experienced golfer ignores the water and sees only the green. His golf ball still goes into the water, but he figures, what the hell, it was worth a shot.

Golfers complained about a lake in the middle of the golf course because they were hitting so many balls into it, so management filled it and made it into a green. Now nobody hits it.

"You didn't count your strokes for the two golf balls you hit into the lake," a husband informed his wife.

"And I'm not going to count them," his wife replied.

"Why not?" he asked.

"Because I left them there," she replied.

A water ball is an old golf ball we use in place of a good golf ball whenever we have to hit over water. It is called a water ball because that is where we are sure it is going.

Never take advice from a golfer who pulls out a water ball every time he sees water.

My doctor is a golfer. I asked him if he had any suggestions that would help my golf swing. He said to hit two buckets of balls and call him in the morning.

A ball that is less than twelve inches from the hole is often considered 'a gimme' that we don't have to putt. I prefer to play the other way. If it's less than twelve inches I figure I can make it, so I do putt.

Sometimes I miss . . . .

"Which club would you suggest I use here?" a wife asked her husband.

"I told you which club to use on the last hole," he said, "and you hit your ball into the lake."

"Well, we've passed the lake," his wife replied. "Maybe it will work now."

"Have golfers in your foursome ever been guilty of covering up their mistakes?" a golfer was asked.

"Yes," he replied. "They've also drowned a few."

"My golf game is constantly changing."
"Is it getting better or worse?"
"Yes."

A father took his son golfing.

On the first par three hole they came to, he said to the boy, "I'll bet you a nickel you can't make a hole in one."

The kid hit a shot that landed in front of the green, took two bounces, and rolled into the cup.

The next par three hole they came to, the father said, "I'll bet you another nickel you can't make another hole in one."

"Make it a dollar," the kid said.

"Why a dollar?" the father asked. "The last time you only bet a nickel."

"That was before I knew how easy it was," the kid replied.

"Do you ever get excited when you hit a good shot?" a golfer was asked.

"I'm sure I would," he replied, "if I ever did."

A foursome had not spoken for sixteen holes. Finally, after one of them hit a drive to within two feet of the pin, another said, "Good shot."

To which a third responded, "Did we come here to talk or to golf."

A golfer decided to get back to the basics, so he bought five thousand dollars worth of new golf equipment.

"What would you say if I told you I had just purchased a new set of golf clubs," a husband informed his wife, "and the manufacturer guarantees that if I don't shoot par within five years, that they will give me my money back?"

"I would say they've pretty well sized up the quality of your game by the length of time they've given themselves to get out of town," his wife answered.

I think my accuracy could be improving. My drives are landing closer to the fairway.

A golfer was asked to explain the most difficult challenge he had faced in playing the game of golf.

"Pretending that I actually know how to play the game," he replied.

Some retirees decided to take up golf.

"Sometimes it takes many years to learn the game," the golf pro advised them, attempting to explain how difficult it could be.

"We're in no hurry," a retiree replied.

You might suspect you're teeing your golf ball a little too high when your tee disappears and your ball is still there.

The very least a golfer can do when he hits another golfer with a golf ball is apologize.

"I'm awfully sorry sir, are you all right, I hope I didn't hurt you, don't bother getting up, you didn't happen to see where my ball went, did you ... ?"

Golf is very much like bowling. At least a lot of the scores are the same.

A question on an application form to join the local golf and county club read, "Average Score - if a golfer?"

"Seventy-two," the applicant wrote.

"That's a really low average," he was told. "Are you sure your score is that low?"

"I'm sure it would be," he replied. "If I were a golfer."

"I tried several different sets of golf clubs to see if I could eliminate some faults in my game."

"What did you learn?"

"I learned it wasn't the golf clubs."

If golfers can't hit a golf ball straight with one club, you will often see them switch to another club.

Like it's the club's fault ....

I enjoy playing with noncompetitive golfers. All the competitive golfers I play with appear to hate the game.

Golf isn't so different from work. When it's good, it's O.K., but when it's bad . . . . Come to think of it, golf isn't anything like work.

The problem with shooting a good round of golf is, it ends too soon.

The problem with shooting a poor round of golf is, it doesn't end soon enough.

"My husband claims he made me the golfer I am today," one wife said to another as they searched for their wayward drives in the rough. "I figured, what the heck, as long as he's willing to take the blame . . . ."

"I have some bad news and some good news," students were informed by a golf pro. "The bad news is, none of you can hit a ball straight. The good news is, no one else can either."

A wife purchased a book for her husband. She said it could cure one hundred mistakes commonly made by golfers.

He replied, "Only a hundred . . . ?"

"What would you say if I told you all my drives are hitting the fairway?" a golf pro was asked.

"I would say your drives aren't going far enough," the pro replied.

If you want to know why golf courses don't put their club houses near the side of a fairway, watch a few golfers tee off on the first hole.

When you ask, "Did you enjoy golf today?" some golfers can tell you right away. Others have to wait until they fill out their score card.

How bad was my golf game this morning? I didn't feel comfortable with my second shot unless I was lining it up through tree branches.

The easiest way to get a hole in one: Take careful aim . . . seven million times.

I hit a lot of straight drives in my game today. Ten percent went straight down the fairway, and ninety percent went straight into the rough.

I once hit a drive four hundred yards. My ball would have gone even farther if that cart path hadn't turned.

I always know when my husband has had a bad golf game. His first words when he comes through the door are, "Don't ask!"

"How are you doing?" one golfer asked another.

"Not bad," the other golfer replied. "So far I've had sixteen pars and a birdie."

"Wow!" the first golfer exclaimed. "I'm impressed. I don't meet too many golfers who play that well in a game."

"Oh, I didn't know you meant this game," the other golfer said. "I thought you meant since I began golfing."

"I almost hit something with a golf ball today," a dejected golfer informed another golfer.

"Really," the other golfer replied with a slightly worried look. "What?"

"A fairway," the dejected golfer answered.

A bowler and a golfer were arguing about who was the better at their sport.

"Even with my worst slice, I've never lost a ball," the bowler said.

"That might be true," the golfer replied, "but then you also have someone who finds them and returns them to you."

AN ECONOMICAL WAY TO
PERFECT YOUR SWING AND LEARN
HOW TO HIT A GOLF BALL

Equipment required:

  (a)   One light weight practice golf ball.
  (b)   One golf club.
  ©)   One back yard.
  (d)   One house (a side with no windows).
  (e)   Lots of repetition.

A practice golf ball is the same size as a real golf ball, except it is made out of lighter materials such as plastic or sponge and will not travel as far. It is used mainly to practice the golf swing in the back yard. The nice thing about a practice ball is that it reacts in much the same way as a real ball on a golf course and will go in virtually any direction it is aimed, or not aimed.

A golf course is not required to learn the golf swing. Neither is a driving range. All you really need is a back yard, and of course the light weight practice ball. It will help if your yard is at least twenty-five yards in length to allow for your long drives, and a hundred yards wide to accommodate the other shots you will be making.

I found my five iron to be a good club with

which to practice. When I used my nine iron or pitching wedge the practice ball went over the house, and when I used my three iron or driver my wife was afraid to stay in the kitchen. Keep in mind that lower numbered clubs are the most difficult to control accuracy, next to the putter of course.

A building (a side with no windows) is a good target. To increase your confidence, try aiming at one you can hit, such as a large house, or a barn, or a forty-story apartment complex. You could also try using a city park, although it is not recommended. My wife sometimes becomes upset when she sees me hitting practice balls off the lush green grass in the park, especially since it disturbs our dog and prevents him from going to the bathroom.

Repetition is really what the swing is all about and is one part of the game that you can easily learn in your back yard with the practice ball. If you still think you would rather be on the driving range at the golf course, try counting the cost for each ball that is hit - three cents, six cents, nine cents, or whatever the course charges for a bucket of balls. After eighty or ninety thousand swings you will begin to realize that back yard golf with a practice ball is a real bargain. For myself, by using the practice ball, I would estimate that even after subtracting the cost of windows, I have saved somewhere in the area of twelve million dollars.

Learning to avoid obstacles:

Lakes can be very intimidating. For some reason, whenever we see a lake on a golf course, we are drawn to hit our golf ball into it. To learn how to hit over or around lakes, you might try placing a bucket of water in the middle of your back yard and practice hitting over and around it with your practice ball. Keep practicing until you eventually miss the bucket.

Trees along the fairways are much like lakes and are difficult to miss. Any time there are trees, there is a good chance your ball will end up behind one. As with a real golf ball, I have found the best way to miss a tree with my practice ball is to aim for it.

Sand traps can be troublesome and at first you will not be able to practice hitting your practice ball out of them in your back yard. But be patient. After you have taken a few thousand divots out of your lawn, there is a good possibility your entire yard will be a sand trap.

Fortunately, hitting golf balls out of the rough is one shot that you will not have to learn in the back yard with your practice ball since, thanks to the slice and the hook, you will be getting plenty of practice hitting these shots on the golf course during your regular game.

The slice and the hook are the two easiest shots to hit in golf. How to tell the difference between a slice and a hook? If your practice ball is landing in your neighbor's yard, it is probably a slice. If your practice ball is landing in your other neighbor's yard, it is probably a hook.

To learn how to hit your ball straight, perhaps have someone you know examine your swing and offer suggestions. Many wives choose their husbands, since they will be doing it anyway and will probably continue to do it for the rest of their lives. For my wife, she has found that if I stand against the house and watch her practice ball careening directly toward me, it improves her aim tremendously.

You will find that through repetition, once you have learned to repeat the same swing every time with your practice ball, it will not be nearly as difficult to get your real golf ball to go straight every time in a regular game, or at least in the same general direction every time, or at least some of the time.

****

"It's kind of sad watching a man when he realizes he will never be a great golfer," one golf pro said to another.

"Really?" the other golf pro replied. "I've never seen one of those."

A wife was golfing by herself.

"Where's your husband?" she was asked.

"Oh, he hit a golf ball into a family's yard beside the third fairway and went in to look for it," she explained.

"Does he always take this long to find a lost ball?" she was asked.

"No," she replied. "He has usually found his ball, hit it back to the fairway, discussed his game with the owner, filled out police reports, and returned by now."

Wouldn't it be nice if we could golf as good as our score card says we golfed.

"I suppose the game of golf is like everything else we do in life. We're just as good as we think we are."

"Why is everybody laughing?"

The main difference between a difficult golf course and an easy golf course? The golfer.

A golf pro was questioning a golfer about her knowledge of the game.

"What do you say to someone who hits your golf ball by mistake?" he asked.

"I don't say anything," she replied, "until I see where it lands."

Why is it, the narrower the fairways, the more difficult the roughs, the deeper the sand traps, the more numerous the lakes . . . the higher the cost is to play. You'd think we'd get a break in the price for those conditions.

If you really want to have a bad game of golf, just tell another golfer how good you are.

The difference between a low score on a hole and a high score on a hole is proportional to the amount of times a golfer has to mentally retrace his steps to calculate the number of strokes he has taken on the hole.

"I can tell a golfer is upset after a game by the language he uses," one golf pro said to another.

"You mean, like cuss words . . . ?" the second golf pro asked.

"No," the first golf pro replied. "I mean, like bogey, double bogey, triple bogey . . . ."

"My wife lets me golf anytime I like," one golfer informed another.

"She doesn't mind?" the other golfer asked.

"Not at all," the first golfer answered.

"Don't you ever wonder what she's doing while you're out golfing?" the other golfer asked.

"Not so far," the first golfer replied. "That's her over on the first tee."

If golf is supposed to be therapeutic, why do so many golfers look like they could use therapy.

A golfer sliced three drives into a lake.

"Why did you hit so many, when you knew they were going to go there?" another golfer asked.

The golfer shrugged. "For the first hundred and fifty yards they looked O.K."

"It was awfully nice of that gentleman to stay and talk to me about golf after everyone else had left," a golfer said to his wife. "I wonder why he did that."

"I suspect he didn't know how to get away," his wife answered.

I have enough money saved to last me the rest of my life ... or I might take up golf.

What do you call a golfer who has difficulty hitting a ball straight?

Average.

I discovered a really nice golf swing in my game this morning. Unfortunately, it belonged to another golfer in our foursome.

"Did you know that when you swing just right, your hands don't hurt and your club head hardly makes a sound when it connects with the ball?"

"Really? I have never experienced that."

"I think the easiest shot for you to make here," one golfer said to another, "would be a slight draw around that thicket of trees between your ball and the green."

"If I had the skills to hit a slight draw around that thicket of trees," the golfer replied, "that thicket of trees wouldn't be between my ball and the green in the first place."

By using an advanced computer technology program, a golf pro was able to show me the score I could expect after completing my lessons.

I liked it. According to the computer, I was thirty-seven under par.

"Why are there nine or eighteen holes in golf instead of ten or twenty holes?"

"It was invented before the metric system."

"This essay describing your father's golf game is exactly the same as the stories handed in by three other students," a teacher said.

"I know," the student answered. "They were all in the same foursome."

A soccer player took up golf. He liked it because he was able to use many of the same skills, like kicking the ball.

If you want to see real happiness, just watch a wife's face when her husband asks if he can go golfing Saturday morning. After he goes golfing, she goes shopping.

Two golfers were in the rough, searching for their wayward drives.

"Is this one yours?" one of them asked, pointing toward a ball.

The other golfer examined the ball, then broke into a broad smile.

"Why, yes it is, thank you very much," she exclaimed. "Now, could you also help me find the ball I lost today."

Two golfers met in the rough.

"I don't think I'm doing very well today," one of them said.

The other nodded. "That makes seventy-two of us."

"The game of golf might appear easy on paper," one golfer said to another, "but it is very difficult in practice."

"I know," the other golfer replied. "I've watched you play and then read your score card."

Golfers were introducing themselves on the first tee.

"How do you feel about listening to a lot of cussing and swearing?" asked one.

"It doesn't bother me at all," answered another.

"Good," replied the golfer who had asked the question. "How would you like to telephone my wife and tell her where I am."

I informed my wife that she could deduct the occasional stroke on longer fairways. On one hole she deducted a mulligan, two practice shots, three ground under repair rules, and a stroke for a tree that shouldn't have been there.

I think my wife might be angry with me. The sky was filled with lightning when I said I was going golfing, and she suggested I take my extra long driver.

"How many strokes did it take you on that hole?" a husband asked his wife.

"Five," she replied.

"Including getting out of the sand trap?" he asked.

"Oh, all right . . . ten."

"I've got it," a husband exclaimed to his wife. "I've finally discovered the perfect swing. I'll never again miss a fairway."

"That's nice dear," answered his wife. "Now will you please put away your golf clubs and come back to bed."

A wife returned home from her first golf lesson.

"How did you do?" her husband asked.

"I did very well," she replied. "Our instructor said that as golf games go, my score would be considerably above average."

I like golf. It's playing the damned game that drives me crazy.

A husband answered the telephone, made some calls, then hurriedly got dressed to go out.

His wife stared at the torrents of wind and rain that were hitting the house. "Where do you think you're going in this weather?" she asked.

"It's Jim," he replied, referring to one of his golfing buddies. "They say he's gone insane. He paid for an, all you can play, tee time at that new golf and country club that just opened, and now he refuses to come off the course. They want me to see what I can do."

His wife stared again at the wind and rain. "If he's as crazy as they say he is, you'd better take someone to help you."

"I've already called Bill and George," he said. "I'm picking them up on the way."

"Do you think three of you will be able to handle him?" she asked.

"Handle him!" he scoffed. "We're not going to handle him! We're going to play with him!"

Have you ever wondered what professional golfers do when they retire?

After his first lesson, a teenager was asked by his mother how he enjoyed golfing.

"Not much," he replied. "I'm sorry I even bothered learning the game."

84

I asked my husband what he would like for his birthday. He said he wanted his golf clubs upgraded. So I had the electrical tape on his grips replaced.

"My husband and I played golf today with a man who wouldn't stop swearing," one wife said to another.

"Were you offended?" the other wife asked.

"Yes I was," the first wife replied.

"What about your husband?" the other wife asked. "Was he offended?"

"No," the first wife replied. "He thought the other golfer was just trying to tell us where his ball went."

A golfer hit a beautiful shot that sailed two hundred and fifty yards, passed over a body of water, and landed squarely in the middle of the green.

After congratulations from the other golfers in his foursome had subsided, he said, "It wasn't a bad shot, considering my intention was to lay up on this side of the water."

"I was all tensed up, so I decided to come golfing to relax . . . . Did anybody see where my #%$^&%$# ball went . . . ?"

"There is a lot of drama in golf," a golfer announced, coming to the defense of the game.

"You mean like a Broadway play?" he was asked.

"I suppose," he said.

"And which would your game be?" he was asked. "A comedy or a tragedy?"

Another golfer interrupted, "Both."

"My husband offered to take me golfing," one wife said to another.

"I didn't know he hated you that much," the other wife answered.

A wife, who had dropped many hints to her husband to take her golfing, heard that one of the other golfers had taken his wife.

"Mary goes golfing with her husband," she said, "and I think I should at least be able to expect the same."

The next morning on the golf course, her husband met Mary's husband. "I don't know why," he said, "but for some reason my wife expects you to take her golfing."

If you're looking for sympathy for your poor game, don't expect to get it from the golfer in the rough beside you.

"What causes me to hit my golf ball into a lake?" a student asked a golf pro.

"For some reason, golf balls just like to go there," the pro answered.

"Then what causes me to hit my golf ball into the rough?" the student asked.

"For some reason, golf balls like to go there too," the pro said.

"What if my golf ball could make a choice between going into the rough or a lake?" the student asked.

"Your golf ball would never go into the rough when it has a lake to go into," the pro replied.

"I'd like to purchase a new set of clubs for my husband's golf game on Saturday," a wife said to a clerk in the pro shop.

"And what kind of clubs would your husband prefer?" the clerk asked.

"I don't think it will make any difference," the wife replied. "He doesn't even know yet that I'm going with him."

A golfer was describing the game he had just completed to another golfer.

When he finished his story, the other golfer said, "Say, that was really good. Do you mind if I use it to describe my next golf game?"

I asked my husband to teach me his golf swing. He wanted to know which one I would like to learn first.

A golfer was asked, "What is the difference between shooting a seventy-six instead of a seventy-two, and shooting a hundred and twelve instead of a hundred and eight?"

The golfer replied, "With the first there's a lot of difference. With the latter there's absolutely no difference."

Wives were discussing their husbands' golf games.

"My husband is happiest when he plays well," one of them said. "He only gets upset when he loses."

"Is that often?" another wife asked.

"No," the first wife answered. "Fortunately, the other men in his foursome play just about as well as he does."

At the completion of a game, a beginner asked the others in his foursome if they could tell him how long it normally took to become a great golfer.

"Yes," one of them replied, "About an hour and a half in the club house and three beers."

We had a wee bit of wind and rain on the golf course today. Fortunately, it calmed down a little while the eye passed through.

My wife decided to take golf lessons. It took her a while. She couldn't find a golf pro with a swing she liked.

One of the nicest compliments I have been given was from another golfer who said I could be really good with a little more practice. The compliment would have been even nicer if I hadn't been playing for ten years.

Slicing is a lot like yawning. Once we see another golfer do it, we have to do it.

"You want to try to play within yourself," a golf pro said to a golfer.

"What does that mean?" the golfer asked.

"It means you shouldn't try to play better than you actually are," the golf pro explained.

The golfer thought for a moment. "I think I'm already doing that."

First golfer: "I believe I beat you by two strokes this morning."

Second golfer: "I don't think so. I believe I beat you by one stroke."

First golfer: "But I had the lower score."

Second golfer: "But I was looking after the score card."

"I played golf with three men today," one woman said to another, "and every time I stepped up to my ball, they told me which club to use."

"I would think you would be grateful for the help they tried to give you," the other woman replied.

"I would," the first woman answered, "except each one picked a different club."

A Florida golfer and an Arizona golfer were comparing golf courses.

"We have a lot of ducks on our course," the Arizona golfer said, "and they can be a real nuisance at times. Do you have many ducks on your course?"

"Can't say that we do," the Florida golfer replied. "Nothing like ducks. All we have are alligators."

"If my first drive hits a tree and bounces back onto the tee box, do I have to take a stroke, or is it O.K. if I just start over?"

"Can too much golf be bad for a person?" a wife was asked as her husband left for the course with his golfing buddies.

"It depends," she said.

"On what?" she was asked.

"On what time he comes home from doing it," she replied.

One golf instruction book promised to lower my score by at least five strokes. Another promised seven strokes. A third promised ten strokes. Still another promised twelve strokes. I bought them all. I figured I could use the thirty-four strokes.

A golfer asked if he could play in the foursome that followed his ex-wife's foursome.

When asked why, he answered, "It improves my aim."

Ten thousand years ago, a spaceship was sent on a mission to earth to determine if there was intelligent life there.

After watching the inhabitants hunt for food with their crude prehistoric weapons, they decided there wasn't, so they left. Ten thousand years later a spaceship returned on a similar mission and landed beside a golf course.

After witnessing a golfer slice a drive into the rough and then seeing the birds take flight, the captain of the spaceship wrote in his log, "Nothing has changed. They're still hunting with a stick and a rock."

Salesmen were on the first tee at two o'clock in the afternoon.

"How's business?" one asked.

"Great," the other replied.

The first salesman nodded. "Stinks for me too. Do you want to tee off, or will I?"

A horticulturist took up golf. He looked forward to his ball going into the rough.

Husband: "Can I go golfing on Saturday? All the other husbands are going."
Wife: "You're sounding more like the kids every day."

A foursome suspected another golfer might be new to the game when they heard him say to his caddie, "Give me that long thing there that hits the ball the farthest."

Golfers like to play in the higher elevations of the mountains because their ball travels farther in the thinner air. Hitting it off the side of a mountain doesn't hurt either.

"My wife said she would like to share more interests with me," one husband said to another, "so I took her golfing."
"Was she surprised?" the other husband asked.
"A little," the first husband replied. "She thought we were going shopping."

"Is that new golfer you invited to play in your foursome any good?" one golfer asked another.
"He must be," the other golfer replied. "The rest of us had to play twice as good just to get the same score he got."

"No matter how badly I play golf, I still like it more than working," one golfer said to another.

"You must have hated work a lot," the other golfer replied.

It's not whether we win or lose at golf, it's how we play the game.

If that's true, why does winning make me feel so much better.

Winners in golf always seem to get a lucky bounce here and there. Of course if they weren't winners, a lucky bounce here and there wouldn't make any difference.

A golfer was placed in a foursome that included a woman who was raising funds for a local charity. During the round their conversation turned to the used articles sale her group was holding the following weekend.

"You wouldn't happen to have an old set of clubs you would like to get rid of?" she inquired.

"As a matter of fact I do," he answered.

"Would you care to donate them to our fund drive?" she asked.

"I'm sorry, I can't," he informed her.

"Why not?" she asked.

"Because," he replied, "I'm playing with them."

First duffer: "I'm having difficulty finding my golf ball."

Second duffer: "Why don't you put some kind of identifying mark on your ball, like a stripe."

First duffer: "Is that what you use on your ball?"

Second duffer: "Yes."

First duffer: "Do you put the stripe on the ball yourself?"

Second duffer: "Don't have to. They do that over at the driving range."

A member of a foursome watched another golfer hit his ball into the middle of a lake, then stepped up to the tee and said, "How would you suggest I play this shot?"

We wondered if the man and woman we were playing golf with were married. The question was answered when we heard the woman say, "Honey, do you remember where we parked the cart?"

I remember my first golf game like it was this morning, slicing balls into the rough, hooking them into the water, taking four putts to sink a ball. Come to think about it, my first golf game really was like the golf game I played this morning.

Go figure.

When we were teenagers, we couldn't hit a front lawn with a newspaper from five feet, and now we're surprised when we can't hit a splotch of grass from two hundred yards with a three iron and a little white ball.

Disappointment is when someone beats you in a game of golf. Dejection is when they shoot a hundred and fifteen, and beat you.

Dear Golf Advisor: "I am a young woman who has begun golfing with my boyfriend. Although he is a very good golfer, so far he has not shown any interest in my game and refuses to help me with my swing. Can you offer any suggestions that will get him to correct my swing?"
Dear young woman golfer: "Yes. Marry him."

Dear Golf Advisor: "I am a young woman who golfs with three other women. Although I am having a thoroughly enjoyable time, I feel that I could learn more if I golfed with men who are more competitive."
Dear young woman golfer: "I too feel you could learn more if you golfed with men who are more competitive. The only thing you would not learn, is how to have a thoroughly enjoyable time."

A dedicated golfer never quits. Throw his one wood into a lake, maybe. Bend his five iron in three places, possibly. Swear for four and a half hours, certainly. Walk off the course in disgust and vow never to return, every weekend. But quit, never.

"What's the difference between shooting par and shooting one over par?"

"I don't know .... One mulligan ... ????"

I find that golf swings are a lot like college classes. I only retain about ten percent of everything I learn.

I don't know why they call it a fairway. It's narrow, with tall rough on one side, sand traps on the other side, and a lake between us and the green. There's nothing fair about it.

A boss happened by a golf course and saw an absentee employee who was about to drive his ball off the first tee.

"How are you doing, Dave?" he said to the embarrassed worker. Then he turned to the other man who was playing with him and said, "And you must be Dave's grandmother. Tell me, are you feeling better?"

After his first drive off the tee, a golfer handed his driver to his caddy and asked which club he would need to reach the green with his second shot.

The caddy handed back the driver.

"Reminds me of a freeway," one golfer said to another as he looked down a fairway filled with players. "Slow golfers ahead, fast golfers behind. I don't know whether to slow down and relax, or pull out and pass."

A young woman who had taken up golf was having a discussion with a friend.

"Each time I meet an eligible bachelor," she said, "I have to ask myself, is this the man I want to spend every Saturday morning with for the rest of my life."

After watching his parents play a few holes, a teenager said it looked like fun and that he would like to give it a try, so they bought him golf clubs and made a tee time.

"Which part of the game do you think looked like the most fun?" his father said as they left the club house. "Driving? Iron play? Putting...?"

The teenager pointed toward an electric golf car near the first tee. "Driving."

THE MULLIGAN

The mulligan is a free shot a golfer takes to replace a wayward shot the golfer doesn't like. The shot it replaces is not counted. When the mulligan was first used in golf, it was supposed to apply only to the first shot on the first hole.

However, golfers who happened to hit a good first shot on the first hole and didn't use their mulligan, felt cheated, so they often took it on the first shot on the second hole.

But then the golfers who didn't need their mulligan for their first shot on the first hole, or their first shot on the second hole, decided to use their mulligan for their second shot on the first or second hole, or their first or second shot on the third hole, or their first or second or third shot on the fourth hole.

Of course golfers who happened to have a good round and didn't use their mulligan at all felt they should be able to claim two mulligans during their next round. If they happened to have three good rounds, they would have three mulligans saved, four rounds, four mulligans saved, and so on.

That is why, when you play with a golfer who claims fifteen mulligans in one round, you should believe him when he says it is the only bad game he has had all year.

My golf instructor said that if I got in touch with my inner self, it might help my game.

I did. My inner self couldn't golf either.

A pastor who was searching in the rough for his ball was overheard muttering, "Why have you forsaken me?"

"Do you talk to God often when you golf?" another golfer asked.

"I wasn't talking to God," the pastor replied. "I was talking to my golf game."

A golfer in one group was very cautious. He yelled, "FORE," before he hit his ball.

"What is your goal?" a golfer who was preparing to tee off was asked.

"To shoot par," he said.

"Would that be on a par seventy course or on a par seventy-two course?" he was asked.

"On one hole," he answered.

Golfers were doing a little bragging.

"I hit my ball so far this morning," one of them said, "that it didn't come down until this afternoon."

"That wasn't your ball," another golfer replied. "That was a ball I hit yesterday."

"When did you first decide to take your wife golfing with you?" a golfer was asked.

"When I discovered I couldn't keep my head down," he replied, "and also see where my ball was going."

Funny thing about golf. If you want your ball to go two hundred yards, you just take a nice smooth swing. If you want your ball to go only a hundred and fifty yards, you whack the heck out of it.

"What a game. Into the lake, into the rough, into the lake, into the rough . . . . And those were my better drives."

If you want a teenager to get a hole in one, just say, "Whatever you do, don't hit your first shot into that little hole down there."

A golfer was questioning teenagers to decide which he would choose to be his caddy.

"What score did other golfers you caddied for shoot?" he asked.

"Usually in the nineties," said one.

"Usually in the eighties," said another.

"Always in the seventies," said a third.

"You're the caddy I want," the golfer replied.

"What is this club called?" a golfer asked, examining a hybrid golf club another golfer had just purchased.

"It depends," answered the other golfer.

"On what?" the first golfer asked.

"On where my ball lands," the other golfer replied.

Why is it? The more I work on my golf swing, the more complicated it seems to become.

An entertainer was asked if he ever became nervous when performing before thousands of people.

"A little," he replied. "But if you really want to see me nervous, just put me on the first tee with seven other golfers watching."

"What do you call a shot that misses the fairway on the right side?" a golfer was asked by a beginner.

"A slice," he replied.

"What do you call a shot that misses the fairway on the left side?" the beginner asked.

"A hook," he replied.

"And what do you call a shot that lands on the fairway?" the beginner asked.

Another golfer interrupted, "A miracle."

Golfer: "What did I get on the front nine?"
Caddy: "51."
Golfer: "What did I get on the back nine?"
Caddy: "57."
Golfer: "So, 78 isn't a bad score."

I finally shot eighteen good holes of golf... and it only took me three and a half years to do it.

"I can still shoot par," one retired golfer said to another. "It just takes me a few more strokes to get there, that's all."

"How do you know if a golfer is subtracting strokes on his score card?"
"His pencil is moving."

Golfer: A person who enjoys carrying fifty pounds of golf equipment for four miles, but has trouble finding the enthusiasm to push a lawn mower.

"If you have any questions about the game, just ask me," a golfer said to a beginner. "I know everything there is to know about this golf course."
"He should," another golfer remarked. "He's hit just about every part of it."

Husbands were addressing each other by using the names of popular golfers.

"Why do they do that?" one of their wives asked another wife.

"I think it's habit," the other wife said. "Do you remember when your brothers were young, and they pretended to be their favorite cowboys from television or the movies?"

"Yeah," the other wife said. "They used to be so funny. They would aim their little toy cap pistols and shoot. They thought just because the cowboys could shoot straight, that they could too."

"It's still the same," the first wife said, "except now, instead of being cowboys, they're golfers."

I considered purchasing a set of golf clubs called *The Green Seekers,* until my wife informed me, "You have four other sets of clubs that couldn't find it. What makes you think this set can?"

I like seeing an extra wide fairway because it gives me confidence that I can hit it. I still miss it, but it gives me confidence.

Why is it, after hitting a bad shot, golfers take another practice swing . . . like they're trying to duplicate it?

The worst advice I have ever been given by another golfer: "Play your own game."

Have you seen my game???!!!

A golf pro instructed his students to spend half an hour every day practicing their long drives and half an hour practicing their short game. A few days later he noticed one of the students hitting golf balls out of some tall grass at the edge of the driving range.

"What are you doing over there in the rough?" he asked.

"Practicing," the student replied. "I spent half an half hour on my long drives. Now I'm working on my short game."

A husband asked his wife what she would like for her birthday. "A new car? A new house? A trip around the world?"

"I think I might like to take up golfing," she responded.

"Oh," he replied, "I hadn't planned to spend that much."

"I can't seem to find my swing today," a golfer complained.

"I seem to have found several of them," another golfer replied.

If you need proof that golf is more popular than work, just ask yourself, "When was the last time you gave someone a day's pay to let you work?"

Golfers began to suspect a member of their foursome might be new to the game, when one of them said he usually used his eight iron for a shot but had forgotten to bring it.

And the new golfer replied, "Why don't you just use two four irons."

"My golf game fluctuates just a little. Last week I shot a ninety-seven. This week I shot a hundred and eighteen."

"What do you think caused the change?"

"Six sand traps, three lakes, some tall rough, and two houses."

"Why do men like to golf so much?" a little boy asked his mother.

His mother thought for a moment, then said, "I think it might have something to do with inherited instinct. Just as prehistoric man hunted for wild animals and food, today's man hunts for the green and a hole in one."

"Prehistoric man sure must have gone hungry a lot," the boy replied.

A golf pro offered to show his next door neighbor some of the fundamentals of golf, free of charge.

After a few lessons, she said, "It certainly is nice of you to help me learn the game. I'm sure it would cost me a fortune if I had to go to a real golfer."

After eighteen holes of golf through cold winds and bursts of heavy rain, a husband returned home.

"Don't forget your promise to mow the lawn when you got home," his wife reminded him.

"What!" he exclaimed. "In this weather??!!"

After a golfer hit a wayward drive, another golfer offered some reassurance.

"Other than missing the fairway by a little bit," he said, "and hitting that highway over there, that wasn't a bad shot."

It usually takes me two shots to reach a green. If I don't make it with the first two, I usually make it with the second two.

"If I were to decide to write a book of golf humor, where would I begin?"

"The first tee on any golf course."

"Where did you learn such atrocious language?" a golfer who was flailing away in the rough was asked.

"I don't know," he replied. "It just seems to show up every time my ball lands here."

Two can live as cheaply as one . . . but not if they're golfers.

A golfer was hitting the ball reasonably well, except that most of her drives were landing in the right rough.

To help her straighten out her drives, another golfer suggested she place a golf club on the ground so that it was lined up with the middle of the fairway, and then line her feet up with the club.

She did. The club was lined up with the right rough.

"Could you lend me a golf ball?" one golfer asked another.

"Go jump in the lake," the other golfer said.

"If I could do that," the first golfer replied, "I could get my own ball."

Into every life some rain must fall. Some seems to fall every time I make a tee time.

A foursome came to a difficult par three hole that was surrounded by water. The first three to tee off hit their golf balls into the water. The fourth landed his golf ball in the middle of the green.

When asked how he avoided being influenced by the water, he replied, "What water . . . ?"

How many golfers does it take to hit a golf ball?

Four. One to hit it, and three to tell him how he should have hit it.

"Let's see, for this distance from the green I should use my pitching wedge. But my ball is in the rough, which means I need more club, so I think I'll use my nine iron. However, there's a lake in front of the green and I want to be sure I clear it, so I'm going to use my seven iron. But that sand trap also comes into play, so I think I'd better go to a five iron. The heck with it, I'm not taking any chances, give me my three wood."

Why is it? When other golfers drive a ball into a lake, it's just a game. When we drive our own ball into a lake, it's a *$%#&*% dirty *$%#&*% rotten *$%#&*%# crappy *$%#&*%# stupid *$%#&*%# waste of time game.

First wife: "I could have had a par on the last hole, except for my husband."
Second wife: "Really? What was he doing?"
First wife: "He was counting my strokes."

A wife was sloshing around in the water, attempting to crawl up an embankment.

"This is all your fault," she screamed. "If you hadn't sliced your stupid ball into the lake, and if I hadn't tried to get it out for you, and if you hadn't let go of me and let me fall in, and if you hadn't . . . ."

Her husband interrupted. "Did you say I was slicing?"

"Look at this!" a homeowner exclaimed to his wife. "Some #$@&%$# golfer drove his golf ball right through our window! If I could just get my hands on . . . ! Who's that at the door?"

His wife smiled. "It's some guy wanting to know if we've seen his golf ball."

"I think I might have used a little too much club on that shot," a golfer said. "My ball went farther than I intended."

"I noticed," another golfer replied, "Although that building over there did seem to slow it down a little."

"What is the main difference between golfing and bowling?"

"Well, first there is the ball . . . ."

Golf: Where else can we find a game, where the more difficult it becomes, the more people want to play.

"That's the fifth time this month that I've seen Harry doing work around your house," a neighbor said. "How come?"

"Well," Harry's wife replied, "some of it could be my fault. He decided to be hypnotized to help his golf game, and he asked me to go along to make sure the hypnotist gave him the proper suggestions after he was asleep."

"And?"

"And that's where some of it could be my fault. After he was put under, the hypnotist said to me, what was it again that your husband wanted to become good at . . . ."

"My husband is practicing in preparation for the golf season," a wife said to her husband's playing partner, "but I don't think he's ready. His drives are slicing and hooking all over the place."

The playing partner nodded. "He's ready."

When a golfer arrived home, his wife asked how his game went.

When he answered, "Great," she called the other golfers in his foursome to see if he had really been golfing.

I have to stop letting my wife keep score. She can't keep her mind on the game. Yesterday she gave me a birdie, two pars, six bogeys, a dozen eggs, milk, jam, and don't forget to buy shoes for the kids.

"That golfer ahead has a very nice swing."

"Oh? Did you watch him take his drive off the tee?"

"No. I hit my ball a little too soon, and I watched him hit it back to me."

"Your golf game stinks."

"Well, thank you very much."

"For what?"

"For acknowledging I have a golf game."

"Do you have any suggestions I could use to become a good golfer?" a student asked.

"Practice," the golf pro responded.

"Don't you have any other suggestions I could use?" the student replied.

A wife's golf ball stopped a few feet from the edge of the green.

"Which club do you think I should use here?" she asked her husband.

"I thought you usually used your chipper for those shots," he said.

"I do," she replied. "But I forgot to bring it today."

"Then use your seven iron," he suggested.

"But how will my ball react to being hit by another club?" she worried.

"Just don't tell it," he said, "and maybe it won't notice the difference."

"Can you tell me the difference between a good day golfing and a bad day golfing?" a golfer was asked.

"I'm afraid not," he replied.

"Why not?" he was asked.

The golfer grinned. "I've never had a bad day golfing."

We golfed with an elderly gentleman who had remarried after losing his wife of fifty-eight years. We considered asking him what it was that made him decide to get married again, when we heard him call out, "Harriet, did you see where my ball went?"

"Have you noticed that childrens' books contain a lot of pictures to help them understand the story?" a wife asked her husband.

"Yes," he answered.

"And have you noticed that adult books don't require a lot of pictures to help them understand the story?" she asked.

"Yes," he answered. "So what's your point?"

"Nothing," she replied. "I was just wondering if there's some significance to golf instruction books having so many pictures."

A golfer had a poor memory. Sometimes he forgot to add a stroke or two. He was going to try to improve his memory. But then he decided he would rather have the two strokes.

"Do you ever believe you have conquered the game of golf?" a golfer was asked.

"Sometimes I do," he replied, "but then on my next shot . . . ."

"That's what happens when you don't listen to me," a husband admonished his wife after she drove her ball into a lake. Then he stepped up to the tee and drove his own ball into the same lake.

His wife smiled a broad smile and exclaimed, "And you thought I wasn't listening . . . ."

114

"Do you ever pray while golfing?" one golfer asked another who was examining a ball that was buried in deep rough.

"Yes," the second golfer replied, "I prayed just now, but it didn't work."

"Why?" the first golfer asked. "What did you pray for?"

"I prayed," the second golfer replied, "that this was your ball in here and not my ball."

The nice thing about golf is that it takes so many bad shots to make us wonder if we will ever learn the game, and only one good shot to inspire us to make another tee time.

If you've ever wondered why golfers have difficulty relating to others . . . .

"The housing market is down and our company has lost millions," moaned the real estate developer.

"The market is falling and could crash at any time," wailed the stock broker.

"We've had to lay off workers, and might have to close the plant," sobbed the owner of a manufacturing company.

"You think you have problems," responded the golfer. "Yesterday I lost three golf balls, and my game soared to fourteen over par."

A golfer, whose ball was buried in deep rough, called over a fellow golfer to examine his lie.

"What would you suggest I use here?" he asked.

The second golfer studied the nearly hidden ball for a few seconds, then said, "I think I'd use a lot of cuss words."

Two golf instructors met after a clinic.

One said to the other, "Well, how are your new students doing?"

"Not bad," the second instructor answered. "They seem to have the cussing and complaining part down.   Now if they could just golf . . . ."

A golfer was whistling a happy tune, even though his game was not going well.

As he continued to whistle while searching for another ball that had gone into the rough, a member of his foursome asked, "How can you possibly be in a good mood after making a shot like that? Almost every drive you've hit today has gone into the rough."

"It's not difficult," the happy golfer replied. "Before I came out today, my wife said that if I wasn't going golfing, I could clean up the garage and mow the lawn." Then he went back to whistling and searching for his lost ball.

"What do you think causes one shot to hit the fairway, and another shot to go into the rough?" a beginner asked an old timer.

"Search me," the old timer replied. "I'm still trying to figure out what causes one shot to hit the rough, and another shot to go over the club house."

NO, I DID NOT LOSE MY BALL. IT'S IN THE MIDDLE OF THAT LAKE OVER THERE.

"In golf," a golf pro said, "the most important skill to maintain is a good consistent swing."

"And just how do I go about maintaining a good consistent swing?" a student asked.

"Search me," the golf pro replied. "I've never seen anyone maintain one."

"Do you have any helpful comments you need to get out of the way," a golfer said to the other golfers in his foursome, "before I take my swing?"

"Which club should I use for this shot?" a student asked a golf instructor.

"With your swing, I would say about a seven iron," the instructor answered.

"What if my ball was in the rough?" the student asked.

"Then you would use a six iron."

"And if there was tall grass in the rough?"

"You would use a five iron."

"And if it was really tall grass?"

"Just where are you planning to play this game anyway?"

A golfer discovered something new in his golf game.

After spending most of the round in the rough, his ball landed in a fairway. He said, "That's something new."

I'm sometimes asked if I keep track of other golfers' scores when I'm golfing.

Are you kidding. I have enough trouble keeping track of my own score.

A student asked a golf professional if he knew which shot was the easiest to learn.

"Yes," the pro answered. "The slice."

"Every time I play golf, I can't help but think about my job," a golfer said.

"What do you think about it?" he was asked.

"I think I'd rather not have it," he replied.

Golf pro: "I'm not happy with your golf game."
Golfer: "*You're* not happy???!!!"

"What do you think made your ball slice into the rough like that?" one golfer asked another.

"I don't know," the second golfer replied, "but if you help me find it, we can ask it."

"Do you think your husband can reach the green with his three iron from there?" another golfer asked a wife as her husband prepared to take an especially long shot.

"Is that what they call that club he's using?" responded the wife.

"Yes," the other golfer said. "What does your husband call it?"

"He usually calls it a no good, useless, couldn't hit a green if he was standing on it, piece of scrap metal," she replied.

119

A golf professional was asked to explain the difference between men and women golfers.

"The main difference is what they see when they prepare to hit their first drives," the pro replied. "When they tee up a ball, a woman sees two hundred yards down the middle of the fairway, and a man sees three hundred and fifty yards down the middle of the fairway."

"And what do they see for their second shot?" he was asked.

"The woman sees another two hundred yards down the middle of the fairway," he replied.

"And the man?"

"He usually sees a lot of tall grass and trees."

The back nine: The part of the golf course where we try to figure out what went wrong on the front nine.

A bad day golfing is still better than a good day working: You're either having a bad day golfing ... or you're working.

Why do we seem to hit our drives so much better on the practice range than we do when we reach the tee on the first fairway?

Maybe it's because the practice range is a hundred yards wider than the first fairway.

"Do you know many different golf swings?" a golfer was asked.

"If I knew another golf swing," the golfer muttered, "do you think I'd be using this one."

"Where do you work?" one golfer asked another as they waited to tee off.

"Over at the federal minimum security prison," the other golfer answered.

"Security guard?" the first golfer asked.

"Prisoner," the other golfer replied.

"I sometimes hear manufacturers claim to have the longest ball," a bystander said to a golfer. "Do you know who made the longest ball in your foursome?"

"Yes," the golfer answered. "Whoever made the ball that Big Louie is hitting."

"Would you want to play with golfers who cheat, and cuss, and lie about their scores, and are always in a bad mood because they don't play very well?" a husband asked a group of wives.

"Of course not," one of the wives responded.

The husband turned to the other husbands in the group. "We were right. They don't want to play with us."

A husband was reading a golf magazine.

"It says here," he said to his wife, "that golf is ninety percent mental and only ten percent physical."

"That can't be true," his wife answered.

"Why not?" he asked.

"Because if it were," she said, "I'd be beating you."

An automobile designer decided to use his expertise to design a golf club. The first day he tested it, he took along a couple of co-workers.

"Not bad," one of the co-workers said after watching the designer's first drive, "but I think you need a little more horse power."

"A front end alignment wouldn't hurt either," the other co-worker added.

First golfer: "I used to golf in a foursome of men, but then I decided I would be much happier golfing with my wife."
Second golfer: "What made you decide that?"
First golfer: "My wife."

A golfer was asked, "Have you ever taken a mulligan, golfing?"

He replied, "I don't even know anyone named Mulligan."

"Let's say," a golf instructor said, "that you and another golfer have both driven your golf balls deep into the rough, and that when you get to them, one of the balls is sitting nicely up on the grass while the other is buried, but you can't see the markings on either ball to tell which belongs to you and which belongs to the other golfer. What would you do?"

"I'd hit the ball that's sitting up," the student replied, "unless of course, the other golfer gets to it first."

The best way to discover whether you will enjoy golf is to play a few thousand rounds.

Nothing can make a golfer forget a bad shot faster than a good shot.

"What do you do if you forget the number of strokes you've taken while playing a hole?" a husband asked his wife who had recently taken up golf.

"I give myself a birdie," she answered.

"But how does that let you know your real score?" he asked.

"It doesn't," she replied. "I just mention it to the others in my foursome, and they let me know my real score."

The secret to good golf is the swing. Take a few and you'll realize why they call it a secret.

First golfer: "I went into that yard over there to get my ball, and the home owner gave me two seconds to get off her property."
Second golfer: "She must be getting crankier. Yesterday she gave me five seconds."

A professional golfer had a one night fling. When it was over, the woman he had the affair with said, "I was just thinking."

"Thinking about what?" the golfer asked.

"Thinking about what we should do if I become pregnant," she responded.

The golfer closed his eyes.

"What are you doing?" she asked.

"Praying," he said.

"Praying for what?" she asked.

"A mulligan," he replied.

Golfers in a foursome were looking for a more challenging game.

"Is your course longer than other courses?" one of them asked a clerk.

"Can't say that it is," the clerk replied. "But it sure seems that way."

The foursome made a tee time.

Two genies were watching a duffer as he thrashed around in the rough.

"I appeared before him last night and said that I would give him any wish he desired," the first genie reported.

"And what did he wish for?" the second genie asked.

"He said he wanted to be a golfer."

"And did you give him his wish?"

"Yes I did."

"So why is he still in the rough?"

"He didn't tell me he wanted to be a good golfer."

A golfer came up with a unique way of judging which golf club to use. For her first shot she used her three iron and hit the rough on the right side. For her second shot she used her five iron and hit the rough on the left side. So for her third shot she figured her four iron would be just about perfect.

A golfer who had been hit by a ball was being looked after by the club pro. After making sure he was all right, the pro picked up the golfer's hat which was made of green and yellow tartan with a large furry red ball on the top, and said, "You should never give them a target."

I saw a golf club advertised that will cure my slice, correct my hook, increase my distance, and solve any other mistakes I should ever make in my game.

I asked myself, "What does it need me for?"

"How is your business doing?" one business executive asked another.

"Pretty good," the other business executive answered. "How is yours?"

"Not bad," the first replied.

"Good. Now that we've determined this is a legitimate business expense, let's golf."

The golfers in our foursome have three scores on every hole. The score they give themselves, the score they give everyone else, and the score everyone else gives them.

First wife: "Does your husband have an inflated ego when he's playing golf?"
Second wife: "No. His ego is usually deflated when he's playing golf. It doesn't inflate again until afterwards."

I got tired of making the same old mistakes in my golf game, so I changed my swing. Now I'm working on a whole new set of mistakes.

It was a beautiful day. Birds were singing in the trees, squirrels were scurrying across the fairways, ducks were swimming contentedly in a clear blue lake, and fish were bobbing up and down in the water. Through it all, golfers were enjoying a stroll across a carpet of lush green grass while listening to the sounds of nature around them.

A golfer, after taking it all in for a while, finally said, "You know, this game of golf would be all right, if it wasn't for the golf part."

My wife has taken up golf. So far she's purchased one set of golf clubs and twenty-two pairs of golf shoes.

Just when we think we are finally getting the hang of golf, along comes a high shot into a stiff wind.

A golf course is a place where we go to hit balls into lakes, slice them into roughs, cuss trees that grow between our ball and where we want it to go, lose clubs, throw temper tantrums, get wet, turn shoes green, and have a lot of fun.

Golfers know *how* to hit every shot in the game, but darned if they *can* hit them.

"How did you become such a good golfer?"
"I've *divotted* my life to it."

"I think you're a crappy golfer."
"You're not really certain, are you?"

One foursome was so slow that the manager of the golf course came by and told them to get back to work.

"I don't brag a lot about my golf game. I have a lot not to brag about."

How to shoot par on a par five hole:
Take eight strokes.
Remember six of the strokes.
Then take a five.
Heck, anybody can forget one stroke.

Why is it? A laborer golfs after tax deductions and an executive golfs before tax deductions.

Golfers were bragging.
"I shot three over par today," said one.
Impressed, a bystander asked, "Which was your best hole?"
Another golfer answered, "Probably the one where he shot three over par."

A really good golfer is a really bad golfer who can still have a really good time, even when he's playing really bad.

A husband finally relented and took his wife golfing with him.

"I have just one condition," he said. "Don't embarrass me by telling anybody you're my wife."

After watching him play a frustrating round where he continually cussed shots that went into lakes and roughs, she said, "You know, this is easier than I thought."

"You mean to say you think golf is easy," he snorted.

"No, not that," she said. "I mean telling people I'm not your wife."

Have you ever wondered why they don't put erasers on golf pencils?

I entered a golf tournament this morning, and might have won, except for some other golfers. They showed up.

Scientists believed they had found the gene that determines whether a human being can golf. Then they lost it. They could never find it in the same place twice.

As I see it, the main difference between younger golfers and older golfers is accuracy and how we lose our golf balls. When I was in my twenties, I wasn't a very good shot and lost most of my golf balls in the rough. Now that I'm older, I'm a much better shot. Now I lose them in the middle of the fairway.

I've been training my mind to repeat the same swing every time. For some reason, the rest of me prefers a swing I've never seen before.

"Are you a good golfer?" a golfer was asked.

"I'm the second best golfer on this golf course," the golfer answered.

"Wow!" the questioner exclaimed, then asked, "Who's the best?"

"From what they tell me," the golfer replied, "they all are."

It's amazing, how four different golfers, with four different clubs and four different swings, can hit four different golf balls into the same lake.

Golfers are not beaten by the golf course. They are beaten by themselves. But the golf course is certainly a willing accomplice.

One wife asked another wife what her husband did for entertainment.

"He golfs," the second wife replied.

"And what do you do for entertainment?" the first wife asked.

The second wife smiled. "I ask him how his game went."

"Do you practice your swing a lot?" a golfer was asked.

"Yes," he replied. "But I still can't get rid of it."

First wife: "On one hole today my husband used a driver, a five wood, two nine irons, three sand wedges, a chipper, and a shoe ... and still wasn't on the green."
Second wife: "What's a shoe?"
First wife: "It's what he uses after he misses a green with a driver, a five wood, two nine irons, three sand wedges, and a chipper."

"How many months in your golf season?" a new golfer asked a club pro.

"Seven," the golf pro replied, "except for the really dedicated golfers. They usually play an extra two months in the spring and three months in the fall."

Six pall bearers were carrying a fellow golfer, who had passed away, to the cemetery. On the way, they dropped him into a lake, stumbled off the path into some rough, lost him twice, and then it took them four tries before they could get him into the hole.

"What's the difference between a three wood and a one wood?"

"A ball hit with a one wood goes farther."

"So I should use my one wood."

"It depends."

"On what?"

"On whether you think you can hit the fairway."

"And if I don't think I can hit the fairway?"

"Then use your three wood."

"Because I'll have a better chance of hitting the fairway?"

"No. Because your ball won't go as far into the rough and will be easier to find."

"I like the trees on this golf course," one golfer said to another.

"The trees?" the other golfer exclaimed incredulously. "Every second shot you hit goes into the trees."

"I know," the first golfer replied, "They give me shade while I'm searching for my ball."

I bought an indestructible golf ball. The first time I hit it, I lost it.

"I'm looking for a job," a young man said to a golf pro.

"What type of job are you looking for?" the golf pro asked.

"Something that's fun," the young man said. "Something that's not too physical. Something where I can meet lots of girls."

"I'm sorry," the golf pro replied, "but that job has already been taken."

"By who?" the young man asked.

"By me," the golf pro answered.

A golfer had been teaching his wife how to play.

"Do you think that after you've finished your lessons, you'll retain everything he taught you?" another wife asked.

"I sure hope not," she replied.

"I have some good news and I have some bad news," a retired golfer informed his wife.

"What's the bad news?" she asked.

"As I get older, my memory is slipping."

"And what's the good news?"

"My score is dropping."

"I hit four golf balls into that lake and you don't even seem to be interested," a wife complained to her husband.

"I am interested," he replied. "I'm just more interested in seeing how many of them you put on your score card."

"I hate to be negative," a golfer said to another golfer who had taken six unsuccessful swipes at a ball that was buried in thick rough, "but I don't believe you're getting any closer to the green."

"Don't you have anything positive to say about my game," the unsuccessful golfer growled.

"As a matter of fact, I do," the golfer who was watching replied. "It's still your turn."

Rough: A golfer's language after a really bad shot.

"Stupid place to put a lake . . . ."
You know where his ball went.

When a golfer says, "That doesn't look like my ball . . . ."
It really is his ball, but since it bounced off a house, and the owner is looking for the golfer it belongs to . . . .

A golfer visited a psychic and was told he would have the lowest score of everyone he'd be playing against in his game that weekend. Feeling rather confident, he took several bets that he would win.

After playing the worst game of his life and shooting a hundred and eighteen, he went back to the psychic and complained.

"I don't understand how I could have made a mistake like that," the psychic said. She pulled out her calendar for the day the golfer had visited, examined it, and then exclaimed, "Now I see what happened, you're the golfer. Somehow I got you confused with the customer who came in before you, the bowler."

"I don't get much pleasure out of golf," one business executive said to another. "I just come out here with other business people because it's part of my job."

"But I saw you out here on Saturday."

"Oh yeah, well, then it was pleasure."

A newspaper reporter was interviewing the manager of a golf course.

"How many golfers do you have, broken down by their scores?" he asked.

"Just about all of them," the manager replied.

I think I might be spending a little too much time in the rough. I took a golf ball out of my bag this morning that had grass growing on it.

Golfers were having a disagreement about who had the lowest score.

"I guess there's just one way to settle this," one of them said, pulling out his score card. "It says right here that I shot a seventy-two, and you can't argue with written documentation."

"What was your final score?" a husband asked.

"I believe ninety-seven," his wife answered.

"Aren't you sure?" he said.

"Well . . . ," she responded hesitantly.

"How many times did you add it up?" he asked.

"Four," she replied.

"It must be ninety-seven then," he said. "If you added it up four times."

"Wait," she interrupted.

"What?"

"Don't you want to know what I got the other three times?"

First golfer: "I'm thinking about giving up the game of golf."

Second golfer: "I'm feeling safer already."

"You're still slicing," a golf instructor said to a student, "but that doesn't bother me."

"If you had to go find them like I do, it would sure bother you," the student replied.

Other golfers are always asking me, "What did you get on that hole?"

I think it makes them feel better when they add up their own scores.

The golfers in our foursome don't do a lot of swearing.

However, they sometimes do some muttering, and in that muttering there could be some swearing.

My wife sometimes takes two shots to get the same distance I get with one shot. After she takes her second shot, she helps me search for my first shot.

"What did you get on that hole?" one golfer asked another.

"I think I shot a four," the second golfer said.

"I'd better give you a five, just to be sure," the golfer who had asked the question replied.

"In that case," the other golfer responded, "I think I shot a three."

"So there I was," a golfer informed the others in his foursome. "I was heading out the door on my way to the golf course, and my wife is fuming, and I'm saying, you know, sometimes you just have to be willing to share your life with my other interest."

"And what did your wife say?" another golfer asked.

"Search me," the first golfer replied. "I was talking to my golf clubs."

I heard that a good way to lower your golf score is to compete against yourself. For instance, if you shoot a certain score one week, you should try to shoot a better score the following week. So I tried it.

I'm still looking for my first win.

"What are you doing?" one wife asked another who was throwing golf clubs into a nearby lake.

"My wifely duties," the second wife answered. "I was doing the laundry, and my husband said that as long as I had the water going anyway, I might as well clean his golf clubs for him. This is the rinse cycle."

Duffer: Any golfer, other than ourselves.

"Which shot in your golf game this morning would you say was the most difficult?" a golf pro asked a student.

"I would say the most difficult shot in my golf game this morning was hitting the green when my ball was in the rough," the student said.

"And which hole did that occur on?" the golf pro asked.

"All of them," the student replied.

The difference between a good golf score and a poor golf score: A good pencil.

"I finally found the perfect golf swing," a golfer informed the others in his foursome.

"Let's see it," another golfer replied.

"I can't show it to you just like that," the first golfer answered. "It only comes to me every twenty-five times or so."

If you take a really good look at a golfer and a golf course, you have to wonder which is playing which.

If you think you're the only golfer on the golf course who can't hit a ball straight, hang around some day and watch while they clean out the lakes.

A golfer's head and his body were having a discussion.

"Hitting a good shot in golf is ninety-nine percent mental ability and only one percent physical ability," the head said to the body as the golfer prepared to take a shot.

The golfer's body dropped the club. "O.K. wise guy," it replied, "let's see how you do this."

"Does your husband golf?"
"He makes a living at it."
"Oh, he's a professional."
"No, a grounds keeper."

"This course was designed for golf more than two hundred years ago," one golfer informed another.

"So that's why I've been having so much trouble with these new clubs," the other golfer replied.

"My husband's golf game is getting better. Sometimes he doesn't start cussing until the second or third hole."

The bad part about my golf game is, I always seem to choose the wrong club. The good part is, it doesn't seem to make any difference.

"I told my wife I had quite a few things I wanted to get started on this weekend," one golfer said to another on the first tee, "but I didn't know where to start. She said she really didn't care where I started as long as I got started."

"So?" the other golfer asked.

"So I decided to start here."

A community college offered a course on how to reduce your golf score. The first lesson was dedicated to filling out the score card.

"I'm looking forward to an exciting round of golf today," one golfer said to another in his foursome.

"You're in luck," the other golfer replied. "My brother-in-law is playing today, and he'll provide us with lots of excitement. He hits the ball more than four hundred yards."

"Oh!" the first golfer exclaimed. "Is your brother-in-law in our foursome?"

"No," the other golfer answered. "He's in the foursome behind us."

Golf is a great game for people who want to lose weight. After you pay for your tee time, you can't afford to buy food.

"It was the strangest thing," a husband said to his wife. "There I was, dreaming about being on the golf course, and when I woke up I was on the first tee."

His wife believed everything he said, having had a similar experience. "Same thing happened to me," she said. "There I was, dreaming about going shopping, and when I woke up, I was wearing a diamond necklace."

It was the last time the husband had that dream.

They say that no two golfers are alike.

If you watch them for a while, you'll discover they're practically all alike.

"Have you noticed how having a good lie can reduce a golf score by several strokes?"

"You mean, like my ball landing in the fairway instead of the rough?"

"No. I mean, like later on in the clubhouse, when you're describing your game."

First bystander: "Why are those four golfers huddled together in the middle of the fairway?"

Second bystander: "One of their golf balls landed there, and they're trying to figure out who it belongs to."

One golfer asked another golfer what his score was. After a prolonged silence while the other golfer struggled to calculate his score card, he added, "It really doesn't matter what your score is. We're just out here to have fun."

"In that case," the other golfer replied, "I had a seventy-eight, no, make that a seventy-two."

If you're keeping track of the scores, never put another golfer down for a ten, even if you're sure that's what he shot on the hole. It could prove embarrassing later when you discover he only gave himself an eight . . . or a two.

Amateur golfers have an advantage over professional golfers.

Professionals need to know precise yardage and other measurements so that they can hit their drives exactly where they want them.

Measurements aren't quite as critical for amateurs. We consider anything that lands in the general vicinity to be a pretty good shot.

My first drive off the first tee landed in the fairway.

Another golfer observed, "There seems to be something different about your game today."

I don't enjoy golf. I just started playing because my wife started. I thought I had better learn something about the game if I was going to tell her how to play.

Students were taking golf lessons at the local community college. They were worried about how they would do.

"Would it be possible to just monitor the class," one of them asked, "or take it as a pass/fail assignment?"

"Why would you want to do that?" the golf instructor replied.

"Because we don't want the pressure," the student explained.

"We'd rather not get a grade at all than have to worry about failing," another student added.

"Can you show up?" the instructor asked.

"Yes," they replied.

"Then don't worry about it," he assured them. "If you show up you'll get an A."

If I want to lose my first drive in the rough, hit two golf balls into a lake, take six shots to get out of a sand trap, four putt, and spend twice as long as usual completing a hole . . . I just ask the foursome ahead if they would mind if our foursome plays through.

A wife, who had just stepped up to her ball, was talking to herself.

"Line up your feet, bend your knees, keep your head down, mind your back swing, watch your follow through . . . ."

"Do you always talk to yourself like that?" another golfer asked.

"No," she replied. "Usually my husband does it for me, but he's not here today."

"Why don't we skip the swing," a beginning golfer said to an instructor, "and go right to the difficult stuff."

After being beaten by an elderly golfer in their foursome, one of the younger golfers offered an excuse to save face.

"I would have had a lower score," he said, "but I'm playing with hand-me-down clubs from my father."

"What a coincidence," the elderly gentleman replied. "So am I."

"If you make a hole in one on the seventh hole during this tournament," one golfer said to another, "they give you a new Ford car."

"Nuts," the second golfer answered. "And me a Chevy man."

A husband could be heard muttering to himself in the garage.

A visitor, after listening to the tantrum, exclaimed, "If he gets upset that easily, he'd better never take up golf."

"Where do you think he just came from?" the wife replied.

First husband: "When my wife began playing golf, I did a lot to help her with her nervousness."
Second husband: "Really. What did you do?"
First husband: "I stayed home."

My husband tries to improve by talking to his golf game and telling shots where he would like them to go. Sometimes I hear him tell drives off the tee where he would like them to go. Other times I hear him tell difficult pitches out of the rough or a sand trap where he would like them to go. I have even heard him tell troublesome putts on the greens where he would like them to go. On more than one occasion I have heard him tell the entire golf course where he would like it to go.

"My golf score this morning was the same as Dad's score," a teenager said to his mother.

"There, there," his mother replied. "I'm sure you'll improve."

You won't find too many golfers with an inferiority complex, but some of them sure could use one.

A golfer was staring at a golf ball that was buried in deep rough. She was trying to decide which club she should use to get it out when another golfer approached.

"I'm sorry," the other golfer said, "but that's my ball you were about to hit."

The first golfer took another look at the buried ball, smiled a broad smile, and exclaimed, "Well, that's the best news I've heard all day."

I bought a new set of golf clubs with flexible shafts. And just in time. My body has stopped bending.

The golf course was really busy today. On some tee boxes the golfers were lined up three, sometimes four deep.

Two golf professionals were talking.

"How is that new golfer's game coming along?" one asked.

"Pretty slow," the other replied. "Yesterday I asked him how many yards to the green, and he began counting properties along the fairway."

Two popular ways to hit a golf ball are the high soft shot which has back spin, and the low hard shot which has top spin. Professional golfers effectively use both shots. Since I usually don't know which shot I am going to get when I hit my ball, the difference is often minimal.

Most professionals prefer high soft iron shots to the green. They are beautiful to watch as a ball climbs gracefully through the air and then lands softly near the cup.

My game tends to favor low hard iron shots, where my ball sinks after twenty-five yards and then rolls the rest of the way to the green, or a lake, or wherever else it might be going.

Occasionally one of my low hard shots will skip across the water in a lake and land on a green on the other side. This alone can make it more beautiful to watch than a high soft shot.

The biggest difference I have found between a high soft shot and a low hard shot? The high soft shot makes fewer ripples.

One of the longest periods in a golfer's life is the time it takes a perfectly placed shot to roll from the center of the green, to the edge of the green, then off the green, and into a lake beside the green.

I was describing my golf game to my wife, and she fell asleep.

I thought that was rather rude, so I began to describe it to myself. I fell asleep.

Golfers like almost everything about the game, except the group ahead and the group behind, and the other golfers who make up their foursome, and players who are too slow or too fast, and the clerk who hands out the tee times, and the weather, and the course conditions, and the location of the pin, and their drives, and their putts, and their equipment, and their score, and their . . . .

If we really think about it, what we're trying to do is hit a golf ball the size of a small rock, with a club head the size of two small rocks, that is on the end of a four-foot shaft, that is being swung at a hundred and some miles per hour, by a golfer who performs the function one day a week or twice a month. Is there any wonder we have difficulty hitting it straight.

"I got a new set of golf clubs for my husband," one wife said to another.

"I don't think I could get that much for mine," the other wife answered.

Four golfers were huddled together beside the fifteenth tee. A blanket of rain was pouring down on them, a biting wind was blowing into their faces, and they were soaked to the skin. As they strained to see through the wall of water that obliterated the fairway, one of them commented, "I sure feel sorry for the poor people who have to work today."

Some businessmen were having a disagreement about the rules of golf.

They couldn't decide on who got to claim the deduction on their income tax.

"Strangest thing," an income tax auditor said to a businessman. "You claimed that you paid for another golfer's round of golf as a business expense on the same day that he claimed your round of golf as a business expense."

The businessman thought about it for a moment. "Maybe we played twice that day."

After four putting, a golfer looked back down the fairway, moved a finger back and forth in an effort to count the strokes he had taken to reach the green, added his putts with his other fingers, shrugged, entered an estimated score, smiled to himself, and said, "Close enough."

"It certainly is hot today," a wife said after listening to a weather report on the car radio.

"We haven't even started golfing, and already you're complaining about the heat," her husband accused.

"I am not complaining about the heat," she replied. "I'm just letting you know how warm it is."

An hour later, her husband hit an errant shot into a lake. "Another *$@#%*&$% golf ball in the *$@#%*&$% water," he exclaimed.

"We've hardly even started golfing, and already you're complaining about your game," his wife accused.

"I am not complaining about my game," he replied. "I'm just letting you know where my *$@#%*&$% golf ball is."

"When did you decide you wanted to marry me?" a wife asked her husband.

"When we were dating," he answered, "and you said to me, what did you do today? And I said, I went golfing. And you said, oh, tell me about it."

There are fifty million golfers in the world, of which only a hundred are actually playing. The rest of us are trying to get a tee time.

"My wife told me to give her one good reason why a husband should be allowed to go golfing every Saturday morning," a golfer informed other golfers as he stepped up to the first tee.

"And were you able to give her one?" another golfer asked.

"No," the first golfer replied, "but I'm looking for it."

After witnessing a golfer in his foursome hit fairway after fairway with long straight drives, a beginner asked, "How did you learn to hit your ball so straight?"

"Practice and experience," the golfer replied.

"Where does one go to get all this practice and experience?" the beginner asked.

The golfer pointed toward the rough. "Right over there."

"Are you the person who sliced a golf ball into my yard?" an irate homeowner asked a golfer.

"That was not a slice," the golfer replied. "That was a fade."

Why do they call the rough, the rough? Why don't they just call it what it really is, that tall crap to stay out of.

My husband is an ambidextrous golfer. He can drive his golf ball into either rough.

"Was your wife very upset when you informed her you were golfing today," one golfer asked another.

"Not a bit," the other golfer replied.

"Really!" the first golfer exclaimed. "What did she say?"

"What time are we teeing off?"

A golfer arrived home, grumbling to himself after shooting a disastrous round. He was surprised when his wife, who wasn't interested in golf, asked him to tell her about it.

"Why?" he exclaimed.

"One of your friends called," she replied. "He said you had finally shot a game I would enjoy hearing about."

"And when I finally finished my round, I was four under par," a golfer bragged.

"Wait a minute," another golfer interrupted. "The last time you told this story, you said you were six under par."

The golfer thought for a moment. "Six under par it is," he said. "When I finally finished my round, I was six under par."

If you don't like your golf swing, just play a few more holes. You'll have a different swing.

One business executive's idea of a tough day at the office is not being able to get a tee time.

Golfers were arguing about who could hit a golf ball the farthest.

"I once hit a ball four hundred and twenty-five yards," one said.

"That's nothing," another responded. "I once hit a ball a thousand yards."

"That's impossible," the first golfer answered.

"No, it's not," the second golfer said. "I used to live on the side of a mountain, and when I hit my ball, it went straight down, one thousand yards."

"As long as we're measuring that way," the first golfer said, "I once hit a ball two and a half miles."

"Now that's really impossible," the second said.

"No it's not," the first replied. "I used to be a sailor."

A wife was asked if the weather played a large part in whether her husband went golfing.

"Yes," she replied. "If it's sunny he goes, if it's raining he goes, if it's snowing he goes, if it's freezing he goes . . . ."

"What is the longest you have gone without slicing?" a golfer was asked.

"Four months," he answered.

"Wow!" his listener exclaimed. "You must have been practicing a lot."

"No," he replied. "For the most part, I was shoveling snow."

First golfer: "I don't understand why you're so happy? You just shot a hundred and two, which is a ridiculously high score."
Second golfer: "I know, but it's the lowest ridiculously high score I've ever had."

A golfer's first drive landed in the middle of a lake. His second drive went deep into the rough. His third drive hit a nearby house. His fourth drive missed the course completely and bounced across a street beside the golf course.

"New to the game?" another golfer inquired.

The golfer looked surprised and said, "How could you tell that, after just four shots?"

Golfers were describing the storm that had just blown through, along with the high winds, flooded fairways, and downed trees.

"It was so bad," one of them said, "that we almost had to cut our game short."

"How did you manage to get out?" one golfer asked another as they prepared to tee off. "My wife said she didn't want me to come golfing this morning."

"It wasn't too difficult," the other golfer replied. "My wife was cleaning the house, and she asked me to move my feet so she could vacuum."

"And . . . ?"

"And here I am."

"Everything I know about golf, I taught myself," one golfer said to another.

"It's nice to see you're willing to take the blame," the other golfer replied.

With all the new technology in golf, some of today's equipment is getting really expensive. So pro shops often ask us to leave something of value, such as our car keys, whenever we borrow a new club to try out. The last time I borrowed a club, the clerk wanted to know what year my car was.

A golfer suspected his score might be a little higher than he would have liked, when the golfer who was adding up the score card asked, "Where should I put the comma?"

"Has your ball ever landed on this green?" one golfer asked another.

"No," the other golfer replied, "but it's flown over it a few times."

"When did you first realize you weren't going to have a low score today?" a golfer was asked.

"I believe it might have been during an attempt to hit a shot," he said.

"Your first attempt off a tee box, or your second attempt from a fairway?" he was asked.

"My seventh attempt from a sand trap beside the third green," he replied.

"Another golf club sales promotion promising to improve my game," a husband exclaimed to his wife. "I wonder where all these companies are getting my name?"

"I don't know," his wife replied. "Unless it's from all the payments you keep giving them."

Lately, about the only thing I've hit with my three iron is my golf bag, and last week I missed that twice.

Golfer in fairway: "I wonder if God has a golf course waiting for us in heaven."
Golfer in rough: "Not if there is a just God."

I'm a little suspicious of my new golf instructor. I went by the driving range the other day, and *he* was taking lessons.

A golfer was having some difficulty deciding where to place the responsibility for his poor game, so he blamed his golf clubs half of the time, and the golf course the other half of the time.

"What made you decide to come golfing?" a husband was asked by another golfer.

"Well," he answered, "there I was, sitting at home, not doing anything, and I said to my wife, I wish someone would suggest something for me to do today."

"And I suppose she suggested that you come golfing . . . ?" the other golfer said.

"No," the husband replied. "She suggested I help her clean up the house."

Joe's first attempt went into a sand trap. His second attempt went into a lake. His third attempt went into another sand trap. Joe never could putt.

You might suspect you're playing slow when you look ahead, and you wonder where everybody went. Then you look behind, and you find out.

I'm not saying my game was bad today, but if I were doing anything besides golf, I'd probably be fired.

I purchased some golf balls made out of space age materials. Every time I hit one, it goes somewhere I've never been before.

"My husband just bought a brand new, uniquely designed, guaranteed to eliminate his slice and add twenty-five yards to his drives, golf club," one wife informed another.

"Wow!" the other wife exclaimed. "Do you think I could see it?"

"Sure," the first wife replied. "It's out in the garage with his other ten or so, brand new, uniquely designed, guaranteed to eliminate his slice and add twenty-five yards to his drives, golf clubs."

"I think there might be was something wrong with my golf game. This morning, I found myself enjoying it."

Employees would never think about taking a day off work to go golfing. But they might take a day off sick. Then they would get better and go golfing.

"I don't understand," a golfer complained to his golf instructor. "You gave lessons to another golfer and now he says he's shooting par, while I'm still shooting twenty-five over par. Why is that?"

"You could also shoot par," the instructor answered, "if you did what he does."

"What's that?" the golfer asked.

"Just say you shoot par."

"Has your swing changed much over the years?" a golfer was asked.

"It hasn't changed much," he replied, "but it sure has changed often."

One after another, golfers in a foursome took their shots off the tee, and one after another they all missed the green.

After the last one had taken his shot and also missed, he stared down the fairway and said, "Maybe if we all fired at once . . . ."

"How do you suggest we play this shot?" a golfer on the tee said to his golf ball.

"Why are you asking your golf ball how to play a shot?" another golfer exclaimed.

"Because it's the only one that knows where it's going," the golfer on the tee replied.

How to tell you've had a really bad day on the golf course?

The other golfers in your foursome want to talk about *your* game.

The main difference between a good golf shot in a professional's game and a good golf shot in an amateur's game: A lot of skill with a little luck, and a little skill with a lot of luck.

A clerk in a golf shop was asked for a price on some golf balls.

"$219.00 each," he answered.

"Why so much?" he was asked.

"Our manager used to work in a hospital," he replied.

A wife was asked why she seemed to enjoy her golf game so much more than her husband enjoyed his.

"Because I shot a low score and he shot a high score," she answered.

"What does he consider a high score?" she was asked.

"Seventy-nine," she replied.

"And what do you consider a low score?" she was asked.

"Ninety-seven," she replied.

My wife has been after me to mention her hole-in-one. O.K., so she had a hole-in-one. Big deal. Her hole-in-one sailed straight to the green, took a bounce, and disappeared into the cup. What's so great about that. Anyway, every time she gets to where she had her hole-in-one, she's afraid to mention it because then she hits her ball into a lake beside the green. I have no such fear. I mention it every time we get to the green.

I've had a hole-in-one, and it was much more spectacular than her hole-in-one. My ball sliced over a hill beside a fairway and I was heading after it when another golfer said, "Where are you going?" I said, "After my ball." She said, "It's in the cup." I said, "No it isn't, it went over that hill." She said, "But it hit something, bounced back to the fairway, rolled up to the green, and went into the cup." I went up to the green, looked into the cup, and there was my ball and my hole-in-one. Let's see my wife do that.

My wife did receive some acclaim. She has her score card and her hole-in-one award hanging on the wall in our family room. She was also offered recognition from a golf association. All she had to do to get the recognition was agree to use their credit card.

The manufacturer of my hole-in-one ball does not offer recognition. I keep forgetting the name on the ball but my wife reminds me. She believes it was made by a company called Range.

A husband informed his wife that he couldn't take her golfing with him because he barely had enough time to get in eighteen holes, let alone thirty-six.

My husband's recollections of his golf games are usually better than the games themselves. I can tell he has had a really bad game when even his recollections are bad.

"Wouldn't it be nice if we could get corporate sponsors like the professionals do," one golfer said to another as they prepared to hit their first drives of the afternoon.

"I already have a corporate sponsor," the other golfer replied.

"Really?" the first golfer exclaimed. "Who?"

"My company," the second golfer replied. "They think I'm working."

Wives are lucky. They have to play only one golf game. A husband has to play two golf games, his own and his wife's.

A golfer sliced his drives all his life, until he moved to England, where he began hooking his shots. He thinks it has something to do with the English driving on the left.

"I think my aim could be getting better," a wife informed her husband.

"What makes you say that?" he asked.

"Because," she replied, "during my golf game this morning I hit my ball into a yard beside the seventeenth fairway."

"How does hitting your ball into somebody's yard make your aim better?" he exclaimed.

"The owner said he hadn't seen me for a while."

"Lately, I feel my golf game has really grown," one golfer said to another.

"Maybe it's because it spends so much time in water," the other golfer replied.

A husband was working in the yard.

"I wanted to go golfing today," he informed another golfer who dropped by, "and my wife wanted me to remodel the main bathroom in the house. This is her idea of a compromise."

"When did you quit golfing and become a grounds keeper?" a surprised golfer said to a man he had played several rounds with, who was now mowing grass on the edge of the fairway.

"Right after they told me they'd fire me if I didn't," the grounds keeper replied.

A golf course had several memorial markers beside fairways where dedicated golfers had died during a round. Since Henry played every day and was certain that his last breath would be on the course, he requested that if he should die during a round of golf, that a similar marker be placed where he succumbed. On the day of his death, his golfing buddies carried out his wishes. Later, another golfer inquired as to how they had made out with Henry's last request.

"Not bad," one of Henry's buddies replied. "He passed away on the golf course just like he said he would."

"And were you able to get permission to erect a marker where he fell?" the other golfer asked.

"The marker was the easy part," Henry's buddy replied. "The difficult part was keeping him alive until we could find a fairway that hadn't been dedicated."

"My husband purchased a set of golf clubs made out of material so tough the manufacturer claims they will never rust," one wife said to another.

"How are they holding up so far?" the other wife asked.

"He doesn't know," the first wife replied. "They haven't dredged the lake yet."

A golfer is a person who cusses a golf course for eighteen holes, and then is surprised when someone says they don't understand the game.

Stress in golf? What stress? If we hit a ball into a lake or lose it in the rough, what's the most it can cost us, a #%&#%* stroke or two and a #&%^&*% golf ball.

"He must be really good," one golfer said to another as a third golfer prepared to hit an impossible two hundred and fifty yard shot with a nine iron.

As they continued to watch in admiration, the golfer backed away from his ball once more, moved behind it, and sighted down the fairway.

Finally, after going through the procedure two more times, he called to the golfers who were watching and asked, "Could you tell me where the green is on this hole?"

After watching a member of their foursome try unsuccessfully to get a ball out of some deep rough, one of his playing partners asked another golfer, "How's he doing?"

"Not very good," the other golfer answered, "although I think he might be getting closer to the green. He's switched to a higher numbered club."

"I really envy the way you enjoy golf," a beginner said to a golfer.

"Why thank you," the golfer replied.

The beginner continued, "I mean, to play as bad as you do, and not get upset about it . . . ."

"For our entire marriage my husband golfed almost every day," one woman said to another, "and every evening as we were getting ready for bed he would tell me about his golf game that day, and then one day he suddenly left me."

"I'm so sorry," the other woman sympathized. "Has there been much change in your life since he left?"

"Not too much," the first woman replied, "although it is taking me a little longer to get to sleep."

Why does a golf ball appear so much closer to the hole when we're walking up the fairway than it does when we reach the green.

Have you ever wondered what the force is that turns the sky from sunny to rain during the walk from the club house to the first tee.

I once tried night golf. I couldn't see my ball. My score was the same.

THE SLICE:

The slice is one of the most popular shots in golf. It must be popular, otherwise why would we hit so many of them.

A student asked a golf instructor to describe a slice. "A slice," he said, "is what causes the most beautiful drive you ever made in your life to go a hundred and seventy-five yards straight down the middle of the fairway, and then make a ninety degree turn."

A lucky slice is when your ball goes into the rough, hits a tree, and bounces back to the middle of the fairway. If you are really lucky, no one will notice what happened and you can make believe the middle of the fairway is where you hit your ball in the first place.

The middle of a lake is a good place to slice your ball. You will have to take a stroke and a drop, but at least you can hit your next ball from dry land . . . unless of course it also goes into the lake.

A bad golf shot starts down the fairway and slices into the rough. A good golf shot starts down the rough and slices into the fairway.

A really severe slice is when your ball goes so far sideways that it is farther away from the green for your second shot than it was for your first shot. The good news is, you will probably have another foursome point it out to you. Occasionally, they will even hit it back to you.

Slicing your ball to another fairway is sometimes a good thing, especially if it goes over the rough and lands on nicely mown grass, there are no trees or lakes between it and the green, and nobody else hits it before you get to it.

A hook is just a slice that doesn't know where it's going.

One way to avoid slicing is to turn your club head a little. Every once in a while you will hit a straight shot down the fairway, every once in a while you will hook your ball into a house on the other side of the fairway.

Some golfers make a slice work for them by aiming for the rough so that their ball will curve back and land in the fairway. Sometimes this works, other times the ball will just keep going. That's the problem with golf - every once in a while we hit a straight shot.

A husband was informed by a friend that his wife was cheating on him.

"I know for a fact," he said, "that they're planning to meet Saturday morning, and if you follow them you can probably catch them in the act."

"Couldn't I follow them some other time?" the husband replied. "I have a tee time for Saturday morning."

"Every time I arrive home from golf I find my wife in the arms of another man," a golfer confided to a fellow golfer. "What do you think I should do about it?"

"I don't know . . . ," the other golfer replied. "Perhaps a later tee time . . . ?"

A golfer was about to tee up his ball to begin play on the back nine when another golfer ran up to him.

"I went by your place a few minutes ago to see if you were there," the other golfer said. "I looked in the window and saw a man making love to your wife."

The golfer on the tee pondered the dilemma for a moment, then stepped up to his ball. "Let's see if we can hurry this game up a little," he said. "I have to be getting home."

Wives were discussing marriage.

"And where is your husband today?" a non-golfer's wife asked a golfer's wife.

"He's out playing a round," the golfer's wife replied.

"Oh, you poor dear . . . ."

"I've heard that men consider their golf game to be an extension of their sexuality," one wife said to another.

"I sure feel sorry for their sexuality," the other wife replied.

"Playing too much golf could have a negative affect on a man's physical needs and emotional well being," one golfer said to another.

"What makes you say that?" the other golfer asked.

"Oh, I didn't say it," the first golfer replied. "My wife did."

A golfer was paired with a beautiful woman. After getting to know each other, he said, "How would you like to go up to my place and play another round?"

"Don't you mean *play around?*" she corrected.

"No," he answered. "I mean *play another round.* My condo's on a golf course."

"My wife wanted me to give up golfing," one golfer said to another, "so yesterday morning she tried to entice me with a black see-through negligee."

"What's wrong with that?" the other golfer asked.

"On the golf course . . . ????"

A husband spent considerable time instructing a wife on how to correct her swing. A minute later, when another wife in their foursome stepped up to the tee to address her ball, he did the same.

"I wish you would tell your husband to keep his nose out of my golf game," the second wife said to the first wife after she had completed her drive.

"My husband?" the first wife replied. "I thought he was your husband."

"My girlfriend informed me she was going to stop dating me if I didn't take her golfing," a golfer said, "so I purchased a membership at a golf resort."

"So you could take her golfing?" another golfer asked.

"So I'd have something to do after she stopped dating me," the first golfer replied.

The golfer looking after the score card asked another golfer, "Should I give you par or one over par on the last hole."

"Since you're offering," the other golfer replied, "I believe I'll take the par."

"My five iron's bent," a husband complained.

"That's funny," his wife replied. "It appeared all right yesterday when I was working in the garden."

If you really want to become good at a game, you need to practice. Some days this applies to golf, some days it doesn't.

"Is golf an easy game to learn?" a beginner asked an old timer.

"Sometimes it's really easy, and sometimes it's really difficult," the old timer answered.

"I see a lot of golfers hitting their golf balls into the rough," the beginner said. "I suppose that's the difficult part."

"On the contrary," the old timer replied. "That's the easy part."

Some golfers look like they could use a tranquilizer when they play golf.

For the rest of us, golf is the tranquilizer.

They say your golf game begins to deteriorate after age forty.

My game usually begins to deteriorate right after someone says, you're teeing off in two minutes.

A golfer sliced a ball that went far off the fairway and landed in deep unplayable rough.

"My husband can help you with that shot," another golfer offered. "He hit his ball in there yesterday, so he already knows all the words."

"Every once in a while, you should take some more lessons," a golf pro informed a student, "because sooner or later you will forget a portion of what you have learned."

"Good idea," the student agreed. "I'm sure that I will eventually forget some of what I have learned about my putting, my chipping, my pitching, my swing, my slice . . . ."

"Oh no," the golf pro replied, "you will never forget your slice."

After finishing the front nine, a wife asked her husband what her score was.

"Fifty-five," he answered.

"It can't be," she replied. "I usually don't reach fifty-five until the eleventh hole."

When we hit a bad shot, we should never say we'll never do it again.

Never doing it again only applies when we hit a good shot.

Golfers would make great explorers. They know where they want to go, they just don't know which route they'll be taking.

A wife was sorting her golf balls after a round of golf.

"Good balls and water balls?" her husband asked.

"Straight balls and crooked balls," she replied.

A father took his young son golfing with him. As they waited their turn on the first tee, the boy asked, "What is the most difficult thing to do in golf?"

"The most difficult thing to do in golf is to hit what you're aiming for," his father answered. Then he stepped up to the tee and drove his ball into the side of a house beside the fairway.

"Wow!" the boy exclaimed. "Let's see if you can hit another one."

Golf hasn't been quite as much fun since I began playing by the rules.

"How many fairways did you hit in your game this morning?" a golfer was asked.

"I hit them all," he answered. "Eventually."

A golfer enrolled in a golf class at the local community center.

"What do you think?" he said to an instructor who had arrived and was watching him practice. "Can you suggest any improvements?"

"Four things," the instructor replied. "First, I think your game would be much more effective if you were to take two or three steps before you swing at the ball. Second, instead of swinging your arms in an arc, I would suggest bringing your right arm straight back while letting your left arm remain in front of your body. Third, I would not bother keeping my eye on the ball during the swing. And fourth, I would go over to the football field, because that's where the golf class is. I'm the bowling instructor."

"There is nothing better than a Saturday and golfing," one golfer said to another.

"It sure beats a Tuesday and working," the other golfer replied.

In a socialist country, are all eighteen holes of golf the same?

A golf course was having a thirty-three percent off, water damage sale.

"On golf equipment?" a golfer asked.

"On the golf course," the clerk replied. "The last six holes are flooded."

"How would you judge my golf game today?" a golfer asked another golfer in his foursome. "Excellent . . . ? Very good . . . ? Good . . . ? Fair . . . ?"

"Poor . . . ?" he blurted when the other golfer didn't answer. "Rotten . . . ?"

The other golfer thought for a moment, then answered, "What comes after rotten?"

"Lets say I became your golf instructor," a husband said to his wife, "and after finishing your lessons you were to play golf, and the person you were playing with shot par on every hole and you shot four over par on every hole, what would the difference be?"

"The main difference," the wife replied, "would be my new golf instructor."

"The golfers ahead of us were so slow, I thought I would fall asleep."

"What kept you awake?"

"The golfers behind us."

"I have only one shot," a golfer said.

"Don't you ever slice your ball into the rough?" another golfer asked.

"Yes," the first golfer replied. "That's my one shot."

An elderly golfer was asked if there was any part of his game that had deteriorated as he grew older.

"Yes," he replied. "I can't hit my golf ball as far as I used to."

Then he was asked if there was any part of his game that had improved.

"Yes," he replied. "Now I can find my golf ball."

"You were right," one golfer said to another. "By going to a longer club, your ball did clear the water in front of the green. It also cleared the green, two sand traps, and almost made it to the club house."

"Last weekend, my husband got flustered during a round of golf and vowed he was never going to play again," one wife said to another.

"Really?" the other wife exclaimed. "What happened to him last weekend?"

"His first round of golf."

Golf course managers would like only the really good golfers to play. Unfortunately, if only the really good golfers played, the courses would be empty.

"How would you describe the round of golf you just shot?" a golfer was asked after the completion of a poor round.

"It deserves to be shot," he replied.

Golf is a thinking man's game. Of course, if we spend too much time thinking, we might miss the enjoyment.

179

"I have a question," one wife said to another. "When I choose a club, is it still the wrong club, even though my husband isn't here to tell me it's the wrong club?"

"Did you happen to see a number three ball?" a golfer said to a homeowner.

"Yes I have," the homeowner exclaimed. "In fact, this is it right here, and it broke my window."

"Hmmm," the golfer replied. "What about a number four ball? Did you happen to see a number four ball?"

A wife came home from her first golf lesson.

"Did you learn much?" her husband asked.

"Quite a bit," she answered.

"Did you learn what causes a ball to slice?" he asked.

"No," she replied. "Our instructor hasn't taught us how to do that yet."

When a golfer was reminded that she had forgotten to add a stroke on a hole, she immediately corrected the mistake because she believed honesty was the best policy. She would have corrected the other strokes she forgot to add, but nobody reminded her.

"What is your husband doing today?" one wife asked another.

"He's thinking about cleaning up the yard," the other wife answered.

"Is that where he is?" the first wife asked. "Out in the yard?"

"No," the first wife replied. "He's out on the golf course. That's where he does his thinking."

After struggling to add up the many strokes he had taken during a round, a golfer said to himself, "One good thing, I don't think anybody is going to notice if I forget a few."

A Scotsman was visiting a city in North America where it had been drizzling steady for more than a week. His host was about to cancel the golf date they had planned when the Scotsman said, "It's nice to see we at least have good weather."

If I'm winning in a game of golf, it could mean that I'm playing better than everyone else. More often it means that everyone else is playing worse than I am.

It's easy to spot the really slow golfers. They're the ones who are always right in front of you.

"What do you plan to do when you retire?" an elderly employee was asked.

"Go golfing," he replied.

"And then what?" he was asked.

"Go golfing," he replied.

If we didn't know what golf is, and someone said to us, I want you to take this stick here, and this little ball, and using the stick, hit the ball into a tiny hole five hundred yards away, that you can't even see, except for another stick that is sticking out of the hole, we would think they were crazy.

My wife has taken up golf. It took a while, but she finally found a set of clubs she liked.

She's still searching for suitably colored golf balls.

I have to tell you, I'm getting just a little tired of other golfers saying to me, "Excuse me, but that's my ball. Your ball is back there in the rough."

I like to see trees on a golf course. They provide shade, and they give me something to stand behind when other golfers are hitting their drives.

First golfer who was having a bad day: "I think I might have lost my game."

Second golfer who also was having a bad day: "Well, don't look at me, I don't have it."

A confused patient, who had never been on a golf course, said to a psychiatrist, "I think I'm a golfer."

The psychiatrist, who had spent many days on the golf course, replied, "I know, we all do."

A foursome of women watched male golfers in the group ahead as they scattered to all areas of the rough in search of their wayward drives.

"Well," one of the women sighed, "there goes our theory that golf would be a good place to find men."

A golfer finally came up with a stress-free way to get her ball out of a sand trap.

Each time her ball went into one, she picked it up, cleaned it off, set it on a patch of grass beside the trap, and went on from there.

Learning to laugh at your golf game is a very important part of the game . . . unless of course, you happen to be one of those golfers who actually masters the game.

A golfer who was cussing his game was asked by his caddie, "Do you think all those cuss words will make your ball go farther?"

"Some will," he replied.

"Which ones?" the caddie asked.

"Give me my *%&#!*&^! one iron."

After a golfer said he was putting himself down for four strokes on a hole, another golfer remarked, "And where are you going to put the other two strokes, on the next hole?"

Hitting a golf ball is easy. Hitting it straight is proving to be a little more difficult.

A husband had convinced his wife to watch a golf game on TV.

"See this golfer," he said. "He fades the ball, he draws the ball, he puts back spin or top spin on the ball, he does just about everything a golfer can do with the ball."

"Maybe if he practiced a little more, he'd get rid of those problems," she replied.

My wife asked me what I would like for my birthday. I suggested something that would help me find lost golf balls. She bought me a diving suit.

A golfer couldn't remember whether she had taken four strokes or five strokes on a hole.

Fortunately, another golfer remembered how many strokes she had taken, and gave her a seven.

A golfer, walking down the street on his way to work, was using his umbrella to practice his golf swing. He would hit an imaginary golf ball from an imaginary tee for his first drive, then walk a hundred yards and hit his second imaginary shot from an imaginary fairway. Finally, he would pitch to an imaginary green and putt his ball into an imaginary hole.

"That is the most ridiculous thing I have ever seen," a co-worker exclaimed. "You'll never improve your game by using an umbrella for an imaginary golf club and a sidewalk for an imaginary golf course."

"Not true," said the golfer. "I knocked five strokes off my imaginary score this morning."

"Do you enjoy golf?" a golfer was asked.
"Not the way I've been doing it," he replied.

I didn't have a good round of golf this morning. I took so many shots on one hole, I couldn't remember where I had been on the hole.

"I finally gave in to my husband and watched a golf tournament on TV," a non-golfing wife said to another wife, "and I have to tell you, it made me appreciate the benefits of golf."

"Really?" the other wife answered with considerable surprise.

"Yes," the first wife replied, "but then I always do feel better after taking a nap."

A golfer was asked to describe the best shot in his Saturday morning golf game.

Another golfer answered for him. "Probably the one that took his score from a ninety-seven to an eighty-two."

"A lousy three feet," a golfer muttered. "That's all that was between my golf ball and a decent lie for my second shot to the green."

"Oh," another golfer sympathized. "Is three feet the distance your golf ball went into the rough?"

"No," the first golfer replied. "Three feet is the distance my golf ball went into a lake."

"Do you believe in a lucky bounce?" a golfer in the fairway asked a golfer in the rough.

"Does it look like I believe in a lucky bounce?" the golfer in the rough replied.

"A doctor I play with agreed that I looked too sick to go to work, but that golf might be good for me. I'm not playing with him today because he had an emergency at his animal clinic."

When asked how long their golf course was, a club pro replied, "About seven thousand yards as the crow flies. A little longer as the ball flies."

A husband was giving his wife encouragement on her first day of golf.

"That was a very good shot," he said, even though her first ball off the tee missed the green and landed in a lake. "Try another."

"That was also a good shot," he said as her second ball missed the green by the same amount and landed in the same lake. "Try another."

After informing his wife that her third ball into the lake was also a good shot and to try another, one of the other golfers in the foursome whispered, "I wonder if he's told her where she's supposed to be aiming."

When you say to a golfer, "How was your game?" and he answers, "Not bad, I got a birdie on one hole," you can pretty well guess what he got on the other seventeen holes that he doesn't want to talk about.

"How would you suggest I play this hole?" one golfer asked another.

"I would suggest you aim for that cart path on the left side of the fairway," the second golfer answered, "bounce your ball a hundred yards up the cart path, bank it off a tree, ricochet it off a rock beside the sand trap, then roll it up to the green and stop it about a foot from the hole."

"That's the most ridiculous thing I ever heard," the first golfer exclaimed.

"No it's not," the second golfer responded. "That's the way I played it yesterday."

I was curious as to why golfers yelled *fore* when they hit a bad shot, so I looked it up. *Fore* means *"Toward the front"*.

I think we would be better served if they used a version such as *"Toward the side"*, since that's where most shots go. While they're at it, how about other versions such as *"Incoming"*, *"Run for your life"*, *"Cover your head"*, *"Sorry about that"*, and *"If you don't want to get hit by a golf ball, stay out of the parking lot"*.

Golf is a funny game. When we first begin playing we try to picture ourselves getting a hole in one. After a few games we try to picture ourselves keeping our ball on the golf course.

"Today I become a golfer," a duffer informed the others in his foursome. With that, he sliced his first drive into a lake.

After watching the ball disappear, another golfer offered, "Yep, you're a golfer all right."

An employee in a sports store was packing up equipment to be returned to the manufacturer, when he came across a set of golf clubs. On a slip of paper that was attached to the clubs, a golfer's explanation for returning them was written. "Didn't hit straight."

A golfer hit a drive that sliced off the fairway toward some homes. A second later he heard the sound of breaking glass.

"What do you think I should do?" he asked another golfer.

"I don't know about you," the other golfer replied, "but I'd start pretending I found my ball on the other side of the fairway."

A golfer telephoned to get a tee time.

"I'm sorry sir," the clerk informed him, "but it's been raining for three days solid, and the course is flooded under a foot of water."

"Yeah, yeah," the golfer replied. "But is it playable?"

"You're the same person who broke a window in my house last year," a homeowner angrily exclaimed as he confronted a golfer in his back yard.

The golfer examined his surroundings, then broke into a wide grin and said, "I knew I had played this course before."

"Play sure was slow today," a golfer muttered as his foursome returned to the club house.

"You're telling me," a golfer who had finished a few foursomes ahead of them agreed. "I've never played such a slow course. It must have taken us six hours to finish."

"Were the foursomes bunched up ahead of you the way they were bunched up ahead of us," the other golfer asked.

"Can't say that they were," the golfer who had finished previously replied. "No one was ahead of us."

Golfers were discussing the skills of one of their playing partners.

"A critical aspect of his game hasn't changed much over the years," one said, "which has allowed him to continually shoot a low score."

"What aspect would that be?" the other asked.

"Filling out his score card," the first replied.

Men were discussing their golf game from the previous weekend, in which they had played thirty-six holes and then stayed for several more hours of refreshments and conversation in the club house.

"Did you enjoy yourself?" one of them asked a first time golfer.

"I had a really enjoyable time," the first time golfer replied, "except for all the cussing and complaining."

"I don't recall hearing any cussing and complaining," the other golfer said.

The first time golfer grimaced. "You would if you had come home with me."

"What's the name of your book?" a golfer asked an author.

"How To Maintain A Perfect Golf Swing," the author answered.

"I'll give you this much," the golfer replied, "you have a good imagination."

"I'm always nervous as I stand over my ball for my first shot."

"What about your second shot?"

"Not as nervous."

"Why not?"

"Can't find it."

"You can learn a lot about golfers you would like to play with by observing them when they hit a golf ball," an old timer advised a beginner.

"Will I learn a lot about their swings?" the beginner asked.

"No," the old timer replied. "But you will learn a lot about their dispositions."

"I shot a seventy-two in my golf game this morning," one golfer said to another.

"Really," the other golfer answered. "And which hole did you shoot it on?"

I try not to dwell on the poor rounds of golf I played in the past. I'm not too thrilled about some of the rounds I'll be playing in the future either.

The golfers in my foursome like to help me with my swing. They warn other golfers when I'm getting ready to take it.

First wife: "I'm a little concerned for the safety of our neighbors. My husband has put up a net against the side of the house, and he's practicing hitting golf balls."
Second wife: "Is he missing the net?"
First wife: "He's missing the house."

"What would you say are the biggest obstacles to maintaining a good golf game?" a golfer was asked.

"Oh, I don't know," he replied. "Slices, hooks, roughs, lakes, trees . . . ."

A golfer didn't like his score, so he changed his clubs, his golf balls, his swing, his putting stance, his golf pro, his tee time, he even changed the course where he played. The only thing he didn't change was his score.

A golfer who had gone into a dense thicket of shrubbery after a ball was howling each time he touched a thorny branch.

"Why don't you just leave your ball in there?" another golfer suggested.

"I found my ball two minutes ago," the golfer replied.

"Then why don't you come out?" the other golfer yelled.

"I don't come into a place like this for just one golf ball," the golfer in the thicket yelled back.

They say that if you watch people long enough, you will be able to predict how they will perform in any given situation. This does not work with golfers.

After driving four golf balls into a lake, a golfer hurled his one wood down the middle of the fairway.

It was the first time anything from his golf bag had ever landed there.

So I said to myself, "If I aim for those golfers in the middle of the fairway, maybe it will give me a good line to the green."

How was I to know I would finally hit a fairway.

Men choose golf clubs to hit a golf ball in much the same way women choose which clothes to wear. They pull every club out of their bag, examine it, put it back, and then when they get to the last one, they go back to the first one.

You can tell a professional golfer has hit a straight drive off the tee because he starts walking.

You can tell an amateur golfer has hit a straight drive off the tee, because he stays there for a while and admires it.

A golfer was asked why he took up the game.

He answered, "It certainly wasn't for the conversation."

A wife gave herself an eight on a hole. She was complaining as she wrote.

"I deserve to have half the strokes I got," she grumbled.

"Are you saying you should have shot a four?" her husband asked.

"No," she replied. "I'm saying I shot a sixteen."

A good way to lower a golfer's score is to put him in a conversation with another golfer.

Angry home owner: "I've collected more than two hundred golf balls that have hit my house." Golfer: "You don't happen to have a ball with my initials on it, do you?"

The best advice we can give a new golfer is to just ignore the other four thousand golfers who always seem to be watching as we hit our first ball.

"My husband's grandfather handed his golf game down to my husband's father, then my husband's father handed his golf game down to my husband, and now my husband wants to hand his golf game down to our son. I'm not sure, but I think they might be trying to get rid of it."

THE ORIGIN OF GOLF

Have you ever wondered how the Scots, or whoever came up with the game of golf, came up with the game? What person would design a game where a stick is used to hit an object into a hole that is so far away that another stick is needed to indicate where the hole is?

Have you ever wondered what the first golf clubs looked like? Maybe that's exactly what they were, clubs. After a battle with the English, the Scotsmens' weapons were hanging on a wall, or leaning against their chariots, or wherever they kept their clubs back then, and a Scotsman, after being told by his wife to clean up the yard, decided instead to grab his clubs and head for the pasture to hit something, very much like golfers do today when told to clean up the yard.

But hit what? All the Englishmen had gone home. Now I could be wrong here, but I believe the word golf could have originated from Gauls, a fighting clan that the Scots would occasionally do battle with. Maybe that's what the Scotsman was doing, pretending he was taking a swing at the Gauls.

What were the first gauls bauls, or golf balls if you prefer, made of? When I was a kid we played hockey with road apples (frozen horse manure). Maybe that's what the Scots used. Maybe the road apples reminded them of the English (keep in mind that this was right after they had been in a battle with the English).

Where did the first golf course originate? I would think a pasture that had been grazed down by sheep. The roughs were probably fence corners and the like that the sheep hadn't touched. Sand traps, well they were probably just that, pockets of sand that the owner of the pasture dug for spite to annoy the golfers. Lakes especially could be a problem, what with getting the frozen road apples out before they thawed. Maybe that's where *'Leave it there and take a stroke and a drop'* came from.

The greens? They were probably placed in an area where only the finest sheep grazed. The most difficult greens were probably placed over a gopher hole on the side of a hill, from whence the design of many of our present greens came from.

The greatest accomplishment of all in golf could have been the club house. I can imagine a group of four or five Scotsmen out for a round of pasture horse hockey ball, or gauls, or whatever it was called back then, and they're all out of road apples because they've hit everything they brought with them into a lake or lost them along the fence corner roughs.

"Och noo (oh well)," one of them might have said. "Since we're all out of pastures, I guess now I'm going to have to go home."

"Just a minute," another might have answered. "Didn't we tell our wives that we were going to be gone all day doing whatever it is we're doing here. If we go home early today, they're going to expect us to come home early every day. I know what, why don't we build ourselves a shelter. We'll tell our wives we need it to store our clubs, and we can call it a club house."

"They would never believe that story," a third added. "Since we've played eighteen of these pastures, why don't we just tell them we're playing the nineteenth pasture, and that's what we'll call the club house, the nineteenth pasture."

"And we can use the time that we spend there to make up stories about how great we are at whatever it is we're doing," another said.

And so it was. War was replaced by gauls, or golf. Of course some Scotsmen also believed the word 'golf' was derived from 'gopher' because of the holes in the greens in the sides of the hills. Many golfers still do.

....

England eventually won the war with Scotland because of something an English commander picked up as he watched Scottish marksmen take aim with their bows and arrows.

All their shots were missing fifty yards to the right.

A golfer was asked where golf originated.

"No one knows for sure," he replied.

"I heard it was Scotland," he was informed.

"They were given credit for it," he said.

"By whom?"

"The English. They used to play the game quite often."

"Why would England give Scotland credit for inventing golf?"

"It was during one of their wars. The English soldiers couldn't bring themselves to hate the Scottish soldiers enough to go into battle against them."

"So?"

"So the English rulers started a rumor that the Scots invented golf."

"And?"

"And after that, they had no trouble at all hating them."

When we describe golf, it seems so easy.

A golfer in his early twenties went to a golf instructor.

"I'll have you shooting your age in no time," the instructor said.

The young golfer scoffed at the ridiculous statement. A week later he shot a twenty-two on the first hole.

A group of women had been discussing the possibility of shooting their age in golf.

"I gave up any hope of shooting my age long ago," one of them said, "so I've decided to see if I can shoot my weight."

"How are you doing?" one of the other women asked.

"I don't think I'm going to make it," the first woman replied, "unless I manage to gain a few pounds."

"I finally shot my age," a golfer informed his wife after a mediocre round.

"Really," she exclaimed.

"Yes," he replied. "Once on the front nine, and once again on the back nine."

I won't be shooting anything this Saturday. My wife has informed me that I'll be doing some jobs that have been aging around the house.

"Yesterday I tried to shoot my age in golf," one retired man said to another.

"And did you manage to shoot your age?" the other retired man asked.

"Yes," the first retired man replied. "I did it on the fourteenth hole."

A golfer was having a tough round.

"You're not a very good golfer," another golfer reminded him.

"Thank goodness for that," the golfer who was having the tough round replied. "I'd hate to be playing like this if I were a good golfer."

Why is it? Just when we figure out the breaks in the green, along comes a grounds crew and moves the hole.

A beginner asked an old timer, "How many strokes does it take to get a birdie?"

The old timer replied, "It depends on the hole. Sometimes it takes four, sometimes it takes three, and sometimes it takes only two."

The beginner nodded in approval and said, "I like your method."

I like the mulligan. It saves me taking a lot of lessons.

The funny thing about golf is, you can go without playing for a month and it won't affect your swing. You can go from one hole to the next and it will.

"Some days you're going to play well, and other days you're not going to play well," a golf pro advised a student.

"What should I do if I'm not going to play well?" the student asked.

"Don't golf," the pro replied.

"I shot two over par going out, and eleven over par coming back," one golfer said to another.

"Kind of makes you wonder why you bothered coming back," the other golfer replied.

I've learned a hundred and six different ways to hit a golf ball. Most of them came to me during my game this morning.

A golfer and his fiancee couldn't agree on what they should do Saturday morning. He wanted to go golfing and she wanted to go to their wedding.

Why did the golfer cross the road?
To get to his second drive.

After spending millions of dollars on research to determine whether the golf ball or the golf club was more instrumental in lowering golf scores, a manufacturer reached the following conclusion. It was the golfer.

"I hope I never have to play golf again with that woman over there," a wife complained to her husband after the completion of a game. "Imagine recording an eleven on a par three hole."

"Is that what she gave herself?" the husband asked. "An eleven?"

"No," the wife exclaimed. "That's what she gave me."

If you think golfers don't swear at their games, try watching one as he goes into the rough after a ball. Those gestures and facial grimaces aren't him complimenting himself on making a good shot.

"A birdie in the round is worth two in the lake," a golfer sighed philosophically.

"Don't you mean a bird in the hand is worth two in the bush?" another golfer said.

"Don't play much, do you," the first golfer responded.

Two golfers met in the rough.

"Just think," one said. "In some countries they don't even have golf."

"Lucky people," the other answered.

Golfers are funny. If they're doing really well, they talk. If they're doing really poorly, they cuss. If they're doing just O.K., they don't say much.

It's a good thing men are such lousy golfers, or their wives and girlfriends would never see them.

"Nothing but twisting fairways through a forest of trees, uneven greens, deep hazards, thick grass in the roughs, lakes everywhere you look," a golfer complained to a golf pro. "This sure is a challenging golf course."

"I know," the golf pro answered. "That's why they put it here."

"Keep an eye on that fellow over there," one golfer said to another. "I know for a fact that he doesn't count all of his strokes."

"How do you know he doesn't count all of his strokes?" the other golfer asked.

"Because I taught him how to play," the first golfer replied.

"What part of teaching your wife how to golf has been the most difficult?" a husband was asked.

"Probably correcting her swing when she's in the middle of the fairway and I'm searching for my ball in the rough," he replied.

A golfer who had not played very well was cussing his head off as he walked away from the eighteenth hole.

Seeing how upset he was, one of his playing partners suggested, "You know, if you have that much trouble with the game, perhaps you should consider giving it up for a while."

"What!" he screamed. "And miss all the fun!"

A caddy was about to offer some advice when a golfer said, "What could you possibly tell me about the game that I don't already know?"

After watching the golfer hit his ball into a lake that couldn't be seen from the tee box, the caddy offered, "I could tell you where the other lakes are."

I played golf today on a course that is owned by a publisher of condensed books.

It's not bad . . . the par one and par two holes are a little short.

A golfer was struck by lightning while making a putt. As he drifted toward the hereafter, he was met by the angel of golf.

"I have some good news and some bad news," the angel said. "First the good news. Don't worry about your wife. She will remarry. She is already seeing one of your golfing buddies. And oh yes, they will be able to live very comfortably on your life insurance."

"If that's the good news," the golfer exclaimed, "then what the hell is the bad news?"

"You missed your putt."

When he wasn't competing on the golf course, a professional golfer practiced eight hours a day, seven days a week.

When asked why he became a golfer, he said, "It beats working."

"That's my husband," one wife said to another as they watched a golfer search for a lost ball on a family's patio. "He said he would bring me golfing as long as I didn't embarrass him."

A golfer was a little paranoid.

On the front nine he thought the roughs were out to get him. On the back nine he thought the lakes were out to get him.

An executive talks golf at the office and business at the golf course. His time is written off at both places.

"I had to make a choice this morning," a golfer said. "It was either come golfing or do some yard work. It was a tough decision, but in the end I chose golf."

"Life is like that," another golfer agreed. "We always seem to have to choose between golf and doing yard work."

"Not necessarily," the first golfer replied. "Last week I had to choose golf instead of painting the house."

"I shot three under today," a golfer informed the others in his foursome.

Another golfer raised a skeptical eyebrow and asked, "Three under what?"

Golf is one of those feel better sports. No matter how bad we play, we can always find someone who plays worse. It makes us feel better.

Professional golfers very seldom lose a golf ball. But then, if I had fifty thousand people watching my drives, I wouldn't lose them either.

"Do you have any regrets in life?" a man was asked by a spiritual advisor.

"Just one," the man answered. "I regret that I never learned to play golf."

"That's O.K.," the spiritual advisor assured him. "Lots of men haven't learned to play golf. Not everyone feels the need to play golf."

"But I golf almost every weekend," the man replied.

"What number club in your bag do you think was most instrumental in lowering your score today?" a golfer was asked.

"Probably his number two pencil," another golfer offered.

A husband noticed that on his wife's score card were some holes that she had marked with a zero.

"Why?" he asked.

"I prefer not to think about them," she replied.

A golf pro said I should plan ahead, so that after I hit my first shot, my ball will be in a good position to hit my second shot. My only problem so far has been getting my plan and my ball to go to the same place.

"Watch this," a golfer said. "I've trained my dog to fetch my golf clubs. Fetch me a wedge," he commanded the dog.

"That's nothing," scoffed a listener. "Any fool can teach his dog to bring a golf club."

"Do you want your sand wedge or your pitching wedge?" asked the dog.

A golfer played golf in twenty-seven different countries. It didn't help his game, but he did learn twenty-seven new ways to describe his drives.

"Did you learn about golf by watching it on TV?" a golfer was asked.

"I certainly did," she said.

"What did you learn?" she was asked.

"I learned that I'd rather be playing it than watching it," she replied.

"There must be a lot of bad golfers on this golf course."

"How can you tell?"

"The *fores* are disturbing the neighbors."

My husband said he had taught me only half of what he knows about golf. I told him I was going to leave him if he tried to teach me the other half.

My wife was keeping score. She gave me a ninety-seven. I asked her to count again. She gave me a ninety-nine. I asked her to count again. She gave me a hundred and one. I quit asking.

A golfer was attempting to help another golfer with her swing.

"How do you normally play your ball on this hole?" he asked.

"I normally play it into that lake over there," she replied.

The goal of dedicated golfers is to constantly practice and improve on the skills they have put together during their many years of playing.

My goal is to somehow remember the skills I accidentally put together last weekend when one of my golf balls landed in a fairway.

"Good news," a golfer said to his wife. "I finally discovered the reason I haven't been able to hit a green. The optometrist said that as I'm getting older, my eyesight is getting poorer."

"But you couldn't hit a green even when you did have good eyesight," his wife informed him.

"I know," he said, "but now I have a reason."

A golf pro was giving a student lessons.

"How are we doing in our game?" he asked.

"Reasonably good," she replied.

"Are we having a good time?" he asked.

"It's a lot of fun," she replied.

"How is our putting?" he asked.

"Not bad," she replied.

"Are you still slicing your drives into the roughs and lakes?" he asked.

"Oh yeah, now it's *my* game."

The difference between a golf score and the weather: You can't improve the weather with a pencil.

The two best ways to KEEP other golfers happy:
   1/ KEEP up to the foursome ahead.
   2/ KEEP ahead of the foursome behind.

I got my husband a new stove for his birthday. I was going to get him the set of golf clubs he's always wanted, but they didn't match the refrigerator he got me for my birthday.

A golfer in a sand trap was asked what kind of lie he had.

"Not bad," he answered. "Do you happen to have a shovel with you?"

In golf, I like to think ahead to where my next shot will go. I'm usually thinking about fifty yards ahead of where it goes . . . and forty yards to the left.

A wife, not being familiar with the game of golf, was happy when her husband said he would be home right after the nineteenth hole.

"Our foursome was tied with another foursome at the end of the tournament," a golfer informed his wife, "and the other golfers wanted me to represent our side in a playoff."

"That was nice of your foursome to want you to represent them," his wife replied.

"It wasn't our foursome that wanted me," the husband said. "It was the other foursome."

"My wife suggested an adjustment to my golf game this morning that lowered my score by at least ten strokes."

"Really? What did she suggest?"

"She suggested I come home after the sixteenth hole."

"Have you ever seen a golfer put together a perfect round?" a golf pro was asked.

"Only in the club house," he replied.

"What's the difference between a birdie and a bogey?" a beginner asked an experienced golfer.

"Two strokes," the experienced golfer replied. "Sometimes not so many. Who's looking after the score card today, anyway?"

"Do you really think all that swearing is going to bring your ball out of there?" one golfer asked another who was cussing an unplayable shot that was buried in deep rough.

"Maybe not," the golfer who had hit the shot replied, "but it sure makes it being in there a lot easier to accept."

First golfer: "I think I might have lost our golf clubs."
Second golfer: "How could you lose our golf clubs? They were on the back of the golf car, parked next to the lake."
First golfer: "That's the other thing I wanted to talk to you about."

"Do you think you would continue to golf after your wife died?" one husband asked another as their wives prepared to tee off.

"I really haven't given it much thought," the other husband replied. "I suppose it would depend on which hole she died."

Golfers like to look for something other than themselves when they are not playing well. For instance, I occasionally blame my golf clubs.

My wife has never blamed her golf clubs. She has blamed the dew on the grass, and the heaviness of the air, and the lakes and the roughs and the sand traps, and even a tee for holding her ball too high, but she has never blamed her golf clubs.

"What type of format do you like to play when you golf?" a golfer was asked. "Low score, best ball, scramble . . . ?"

"Scramble," he replied.

"And who is best in your foursome," he was asked. "You or one of your playing partners?"

"Playing partners . . . ????"

And then there was the man who was saving his money for a rainy day.

He was going golfing.

A robber went into a pro shop and said to the clerk, "Stick 'em up, give me your valuables, and while you're at it, hand over some money for a tee time."

The clerk replied, "We don't carry that much cash."

With all the different swings I've learned, you would think at least one of them could hit a fairway.

Before I hit a shot I like to picture in my mind my ball landing on the green, and then putting for a birdie or a par.
I don't recall my mind picturing my ball landing in a lake, a sand trap, taking two penalty strokes, and four putting.

"I hate this game," a golfer complained to his wife. "I never have any fun, and it's costing me a fortune."
"On the positive side," his wife answered, "just think how much it would cost you if you *were* having fun."

"My husband's foursome consists of three duffers and a golfer."
"Oh? And which one thinks he's the golfer?"
"All of them."

After slicing another ball into lake, a golfer muttered, "Somewhere in this world, someone must have a golf club that can hit a fairway."
"I'm sorry," another golfer responded, "but I'm using my putter."

College students were having a disagreement about the rules of golf. To settle the argument they decided to telephone their golf instructor.

"We have a question," the student who called said. "Let's say a golfer's ball lands in a very difficult lie, and no matter how many times the golfer tries, she can't get it out. Would you advise that golfer to keep trying to get it out or would you advise that golfer to take a penalty stroke and a drop?"

"I wouldn't worry about all that for now," the instructor answered. "Why don't you just wait until you play in an actual game."

"I am playing in an actual game," the student replied. "I'm in a sand trap beside the fifteenth green."

Some of the happiest golfers play with wives. They send their husbands to work and then they go golfing.

Golfers would never fudge on a score. They might occasionally take a mulligan or forget a stroke . . . but they would never fudge.

My husband purchased a new golf club. He took it over to the practice range. He wanted to try it out at least once before it became obsolete.

Mother nature is a golfer's greatest handicap, next to the golfer of course.

A tennis player and a golfer were arguing.

"Golfers aren't as accurate as tennis players," the tennis player bragged. "You can't even keep your drives in the fairway."

"We could if we had a fifteen foot fence around it," the golfer answered.

"I'll put my golf score up against anybody's," a golfer bragged.

"I guess so," another golfer answered. "It's so much bigger."

A man goes golfing with his grandmother, his mother, his wife, his sister, and his daughter.

He tells his daughter how to hit the ball. She doesn't listen.

He tells his sister how to hit the ball. She laughs at him.

He tells his wife how to hit the ball. She listens, but does it her own way anyway.

He begins to tell his mother how to hit the ball, but stops when she gives him a look.

"You can tell me how to hit the ball," his grandmother says, "if it will make you feel better."

"Whenever I see a lake, I have a premonition that my golf ball is going to go there," a golfer said.

"What happens when you have a premonition that your golf ball is going to hit a fairway?" he was asked.

"I've never had that premonition," he replied.

"I believe my husband might have been a little upset with his golf game this morning."

"How could you tell?"

"From the way he described it when he came home."

"How was that?"

"*$%#&*%$#&*#*&^%#!"

An angry golfer threw a golf club into a lake, then after a moment of remorse dived in after it. He resurfaced, golf club in hand, but no sooner had he arrived on shore than he threw the club back into the lake. He dived in again, resurfaced with golf club in hand, returned to shore once more, then threw it back in.

This went on several more times until another golfer asked, "Why on earth are you throwing your golf club into the lake like that, diving in after it, and then throwing it back in again?"

The golfer replied, "It wasn't my club."

A woman asked one of the three men in her foursome which club she should use.

"Your three wood," he said.

For her next shot she asked one of the other men which club she should use.

"Your seven iron," he suggested.

Her seven iron took her ball to within a few yards of the green where she asked a third man which club she should use.

"Your pitching wedge," he replied.

Her wedge carried her ball to the green where it stopped near the hole for a tap in and a par.

As she happily strolled off the green, one of the men remarked, "At least *we* didn't have to stop three times and ask for directions."

My wife's foursome isn't golfing this morning. When they heard it was supposed to rain, they decided to tee off at the mall.

A teenager was asked who taught him to hit a golf ball three hundred yards.

"I learned half from my father and half from my uncle," he said.

"Oh?" his admirer exclaimed. "Did they each hit the ball three hundred yards?"

"No," the teenager replied. "They each hit the ball a hundred and fifty yards."

A student showed up at a golf clinic in time to hear the instructor say, "There's nothing to golf. All you have to do is get your mind and your body working as one, like you do in college."

The student sighed, "Uh, oh . . . ."

"I watched a trick shot golfer the other day," one golfer said to another. "He could hit a ball over the rough, and then draw it back and land it in the fairway."

"I could do that," the other golfer responded, "except for the drawing it back and landing it in the fairway part."

"My husband's golfing skills seem to be improving. Yesterday, he played one of the best games I've ever had to listen to."

This morning I played a very nice draw around some trees on a difficult dog legged fairway, placing my ball in perfect position for my second shot to the green. It was even better than if my ball had gone where I was aiming, straight through the trees.

"A golfer in our foursome made only two hundred feet with his five iron this morning. He would have made more, but his club hit a tree."

"Why does your husband do so many funny things when he golfs?" a wife was asked.

"I think it could be because he has spent so much of his life in a dysfunctional environment," she replied.

"His family . . . ?"

"His foursome."

First golfer: "My golf instructor hasn't been able to find one fault with my game."
Second golfer: "Really? Which one?"

At a party, men were bragging about their knowledge of golf. A husband joined in. After the party he said to his wife, "Well, I guess now I'm going to have to buy some clubs and learn how to play the game."

"What score do you normally shoot?" one golfer asked another as they waited to take their first drives of the day.

"I normally average one or two over par," the other golfer replied.

"Wow!" the first golfer exclaimed. "I've never played with anyone that good before."

"Don't get too excited," the other golfer responded. "I'm talking about one or two over par on each hole."

Happy golfers are happy people, and vice versa.

Everything I need to know about golf, I learned from my brother.

I learned that it's only a game.

I learned not to get upset about a poor shot, and to get excited about a good shot, whether it's mine or someone elses'.

I learned that the people I play with are much more important than the game itself.

I learned that the rules aren't all that important, as long as we all play by the same rules.

I learned to respect other golfers, and the golf course.

I learned that the enjoyment we receive is much more important than the score we shoot.

I learned that I really like playing golf with my brother.

A professional golfer was asked what she missed most from her amateur days.

"The mulligan," she replied.

The slice and the hook are what golfers have left after they've forgotten everything else about the game.

THINGS YOU CAN DO WITH YOUR HUSBAND'S GOLF CLUBS:

Hold doors open.

Pull out articles from under bed.

Reach objects on higher shelves.

Stir ashes in fireplace.

Beat carpets.

Support tomato plants.

Pry open stuck drawers.

Mix unknown liquids you don't want your new
sixty-nine cent wooden spoon to touch.

Home protection.

T.V. antennae.

Rodent eliminator.

Dead rodent transporter.

Clothes line - dryer, hanger, rack.

Walking stick.

Lean against wall at front door
to impress visitors.

You can even golf with them.
(Not in that condition, I won't)

First golfer: "I like to get my first good drive out of the way so I can relax and enjoy the rest of my game."
Second golfer: "You mean your first good drive off the first tee, right?"
First golfer: "Sometimes."

Golfer: "I'm interested in buying a new set of golf clubs."
Golf store clerk: "We have several new lines that we can customize to fit just about any type of game. For instance, this set is called the straight arrows, this set is called the long rifles, this set is called the sure shots, this set is called the . . . ."
Golfer: "Would you happen to have anything in a twelve-gauge shotgun?"

"How many strokes did you have on that hole?" a golfer was asked.

"Oh, I don't know," he answered. "Six or seven . . . ."

"You can't count like that," he was informed. "It's very important to keep track of your exact score so that you will know how well you're playing. How many strokes have you taken so far in the game?"

"Oh, I don't know," he replied. "A hundred and ten, a hundred and fifteen . . . ."

Student: "What do you think my chances are of getting a hole in one after finishing my lessons?"
Golf pro: "About one in seven million."
Student: "How come you tell me one in seven million, and my last golf instructor told me one in eight million?"
Golf pro: "I'm a better instructor."

"You just can't teach the golfing skills that I possess," a golfer said to his instructor. "I do it all by instinct, you know. These are just natural talents that I bring to the game."

"Oh, thank goodness," the instructor said. "For a while there, I was worried that I might have given them to you."

Two golfers were discussing the problems another golfer was having with his game.

"I think he could be getting better distance with his driver," one said.

"Are his drives going farther?" the other asked.

"No," the first replied, "but his driver is."

A golfer was reminded that she had forgotten to add three strokes on a hole.

"I forgot to subtract a stroke on another hole," she said. "It evens out."

Wives should try to keep their heads still when hitting a golf ball.

Husbands should also try to keep their heads still when their wives are hitting a golf ball.

A salesman was asked to explain the secret of his success.

"I play a lot of golf with clients," he said.

"Do you manage to win many of the games?" he was asked.

"No," he replied. "I manage to lose all of the games."

A cocky young man who was applying for a job as golf instructor was asked, "What would you do if you were lying six shots on a par five?"

"Don't know," he answered.

"Why not?" he was asked.

"Never had to," he replied.

My husband is using his golfing experience to write an easy to understand instruction book. He's calling it, "One Thousand Ways To Improve Your Golf Swing."

My wife enjoys writing. She says it helps her relieve stress. Right now she's composing an ad to get rid of her golf clubs.

"I was told, to look good on the golf course, you should play with really bad golfers," a golfer said.

"And did you look good?" he was asked.

"No," he replied. "But I discovered why everybody wants to play with me."

"Imagine the fairway to be a clock," a husband said to his wife. "The tee is at six, the green is at twelve, the edges of the fairway are at eleven and one, and the roughs are at ten and two."

"Well," he asked after a shot, "is your ball at twelve?"

"No," his wife answered.

"Is it at eleven or one?" he asked.

"No," his wife answered again.

"Is it at ten or two?" he asked.

"No," his wife answered once more.

"Then where is it?" he demanded.

Perturbed, his wife pointed to an adjacent fairway. "I would say about twenty past four."

A golfer reported the theft of $3000 worth of golf equipment, and a welfare check.

Why is it? I can pitch a golf ball over a green into a sand trap, but I can't pitch a golf ball over a sand trap onto a green.

Golfers standing beside the first tee were discussing the type of day they could expect on a tough course. They were not being very optimistic about their chances.

"Remember that a journey of a thousand miles begins with the first step," another golfer who was a little more optimistic offered.

"You've played with us before, haven't you," one of the golfers replied.

My wife and I share the load when we play golf. She carries the score card and I carry our golf bags.

My husband doesn't think his golf game is what it used to be, but then I don't think it ever was what he thought it used to be.

Two married couples were playing golf.

One couple watched as the other husband helped his wife with her club selection, her ball location on the tee, her set up, her swing, her foot alignment, and anything else he could think of, after which she drove her ball into a lake.

As the two husbands frowned at the errant shot, the other wife commented, "I think he should take at least some of the blame. He showed her how to put it there."

"What do I need to know to enjoy golf?" a beginner asked an old-timer.

"You need to know that if you don't hit your ball straight, it won't be in the fairway," the old-timer answered.

"What else do I need to know?" the beginner asked.

"That's about it," the old-timer replied.

A couple was held up leaving the golf course.

"Stick 'em up and hand me your golf clubs," the robber demanded.

"Don't you mean, hand me your money?" the wife said.

"Look lady," the bandit growled, "you do what you want and I'll do what I want."

"I don't think you mean you have golfer's elbow," a doctor said to a tennis player. "I think you mean you have tennis elbow."

"No, no," the tennis player replied. "I'm sure I have golfer's elbow. All my serves have been slicing."

A chauvinistic male golfer informed a female golfer, "A woman's place is in the home."

She agreed. She beat him by fourteen strokes, and then she went home.

"Let's say a golfer in your foursome took five shots to get to the green and three putts to sink his ball," a golf instructor said. "What would his score be?"

"Par," a golfer replied.

"It's obvious you don't know a lot about the game of golf," the instructor scoffed.

"It's obvious you don't know a lot about the golfers in my foursome," the golfer scoffed back.

My wife likes to golf. She just doesn't like to practice before playing. She's afraid she'll use up all her good shots.

I don't understand, I taught my wife everything I know about golf, and she still can't hit a ball straight.

A home owner, who had a home directly behind the eleventh green, went to the club house to lodge a complaint.

"Ever since I moved into my house five years ago," he said, "golfers have been using it as a target when they're aiming for the green."

"Why did it take you so long to lodge a complaint?" the golf pro asked.

"Because today was the first time anybody hit it," the home owner replied.

One of the most difficult tasks in golf is getting a good tee time.

"We have five-thirty open," a golf pro said to a member of a foursome who called in.

"Wait a minute," the golfer exclaimed. "Don't we have any say in the time we begin play?"

"Of course you do," the golf pro replied. "Would you like to begin at five-thirty in the morning or five-thirty in the evening?"

"Which hole on your course would you say is the most valuable?" a golfer asked a club pro.

"That one over there," he said, pointing to a green that was surrounded by lakes.

"Why is that?" the golfer asked.

"It's where we get our range balls," the pro replied.

"This is serious," a doctor exclaimed after examining a patient who had complained about an aching shoulder that was affecting his swing and causing his score to soar over a hundred.

"Is my shoulder that bad?" the patient asked.

"Your shoulder's O.K.," the doctor replied. "I'm talking about your golf game."

I'm thinking about giving up golf because of my game. I don't have one.

I know just about everything there is to know about the game of golf. Now if I could just figure out how to play it.

I made a little mistake on my score card this morning. Instead of a ninety-seven, I gave myself a seventy-nine. I was going to change it, but the other golfers were really impressed . . . .

A slice is just a perfect drive
That moves a little right,
Unless it turns into a hook
And takes a leftward flight.

Spring is that time of year when everything on the golf course blossoms . . . except my game.

I use a lot of different swings in golf.

I might use one swing when my ball is in the fairway, another swing to get my ball out of the rough, and another swing to get my ball out of a sand trap. Occasionally, I use them all to get my ball off the tee box.

"I think you just hit your ball into that lake over there," one golfer informed another.

"No, I didn't," the other golfer replied. "I hit it into the rough. It had to find its own way to the lake."

I wish other golfers were as accurate adding up their own scores as they are adding up my score.

You might suspect you're getting a putter for your birthday when your children ask if they can measure the distance from your hands to the floor.

"How bad were playing conditions on that golf course, you ask. They weren't too bad . . . once they finished scything the fairways."

"My husband has to decide whether to give up bowling or golfing," one wife said to another, "because he doesn't have time for both."

"Which game does he play the best?" the other wife asked.

"That's his problem," the first wife said. "He's equally good at both sports."

"Really? What is his score in each?"

"A hundred and seventeen."

"Another golfer got angry at me this morning, just because my ball got a lucky bounce and landed on the green," one golfer said to another.

"How could your ball getting a lucky bounce onto the green make another golfer angry?" the second golfer asked.

"He was the golfer I bounced it off," the first golfer replied.

"A little rain would never keep a real golfer at home," a golfer said as he scanned the water drenched course from a bar stool in the club house.

A wife met her husband at the front door.

"Hi Sweety," she said. "How was your golf game today?"

"Why?" he replied. "Can't you sleep?"

There isn't all that much difference between professional golfers and the rest of us.

Professionals hit the ball the same way we do. A little farther and straighter maybe . . . .

"Well, what quality of golf game do you think I'll have?" a young golfer asked after finishing a lesson.

"You know, I was just asking myself the same question," the golf instructor answered.

A wife telephoned her husband from the eleventh tee box.

"Checking up on him?" another golfer asked.

"No," she replied. "I forgot which club I'm supposed to use on this hole."

"Did you hit many greens today?" a golfer was asked.

"Just one," she replied.

"Were you excited?" she was asked.

"No," she replied, "but the golfers who were using the green were."

"Are you hitting many roughs today?" a golfer was asked.

"Ah," he sighed, "if only I could be that accurate."

Golfers were playing on a tough course.

"Just think," one of them said. "A hundred years ago our ancestors plowed these fields. I'll bet they never guessed that a hundred years later someone would come along and turn it into a golf course."

"Oh?" another golfer responded as he took another swipe at a ball that was buried in deep rough. "When are they going to turn it into a golf course????"

A good golf swing is difficult to repeat.
A bad golf swing . . . that I can repeat all over the place.

First golfer: "I'd like to talk to you about the great golf game you played today."
Second golfer: "Go ahead, I won't interrupt."

An optimist is a golfer on the first tee. A pessimist is a golfer on the eighteenth tee. A realist is a golfer who is about to begin his second round.

"I can't seem to find my swing today," one golfer said to another.
"You're lucky," the other golfer replied. "I can't seem to lose mine."

A young boy was showing a friend around his parents home.

"These are my father's golf clubs," he said when they reached the garage. "He says he's going to give them to me and buy a new set for himself as soon as he learns the game."

"How soon do you think that will be?" the friend asked.

"According to my father," the boy answered, "about another twenty years."

"How come you took up bowling?" a bowler was asked.

"Because I'm such a terrible golfer," he replied.

"Have you considered taking lessons from a golf pro?" he was asked.

"Already did," he replied. "Who do you think suggested bowling."

A young man, who had just taken up golf, was enthusiastically telling others how much he was enjoying himself.

"To think that my father has been playing golf for all of my life, and I never went with him," he exclaimed.

"Why did you never go?" he was asked.

"Listening to him, I didn't think it was any fun," he answered.

Attempting to spare a wife embarrassment when she showed up at church without her husband, a pastor joked, "Golfing again are we?"

"Yes," the flustered wife replied. Still flustered, she added, "He didn't see any sense in both of us being miserable."

I didn't have a good golf game today. Some of my drives were so short I was able to describe them with hand gestures.

A wife went golfing with her husband to see what the attraction was.

After hitting his first shot into a lake, his second shot into a rough, his third shot into a sand trap, and his fourth shot over the green into another lake, he said, "And you thought I was having a good time . . . ."

Actions speak louder than words, until you hit your golf ball into a lake.

Then it's the words turn.

Many newer golf clubs contain alloys that allow greater distance and accuracy. Some golfers resent the advantage they provide. Yesterday, somebody let the titanium out of my driver.

"My golf instructor accused me of not being able to do with my swing what he's been trying to teach me to do with my swing. But then, if I were capable of doing with my swing what he's been trying to teach me to do with my swing, I wouldn't be needing him, would I?"

Golf balls are becoming just too expensive. Yesterday a golfer asked me if I would help him find one that he lost in the rough. He offered me a reward.

Course manager: "Did you make that SLOW, GOLFERS CROSSING sign and instal it out on the street like I asked?"
Assistant: "Yes, but I have to do it again. I printed it wrong."
Course manager: "How come?"
Assistant: "I didn't know it was supposed to have a comma."

"Where did you get the bump on your head?" a golfer was asked.
"Golfing," he replied.
"Hit by a ball?" he was asked.
"Hit by the wife," he replied. "I was giving her lessons and stood a little too close to her back swing. *She says it was an accident....*"

A golfer had separated the clubs in her bag according to how well she played with them.

In one compartment were clubs that sliced to the right. In another compartment were clubs that hooked to the left. In another compartment were clubs that hit reasonably straight.

"What's wrong with this one?" another golfer asked, pointing to a club that was in a compartment all by itself.

"It can't seem to make up its mind," she answered. "It's still going all over the place."

I once played golf with a judge from the Olympics. I let him keep score. On one hole he gave me a 5.9,

The owners of a golf course were being audited by the Internal Revenue Service. It appears they were taking some mulligans with the receipts.

Trying to help a new student describe the level of his game, a golf pro asked, "If you were to compare your game to a meal, would you say it was more like a tenderloin steak, a New York steak, a rib eye steak, or a hamburger?"

The student thought for a moment and then replied, "Probably more like a beef stew."

A golfer decided to take another look at his golfing attire when he heard a mother, who was walking by with her young son, say, "No sweety, they don't all dress like that."

Laugh at your golf game and other golfers will laugh with you. Cuss at your golf game and they'll laugh even harder.

A golfer entered a tournament.
The golf professional in charge said, "May the best golfer win."
The golfer replied, "Not if I have anything to do with it."

I had to stop golfing with my wife and her friends. Their constant laughter was taking all the fun out of the game.

The favorite hole for many golfers is the nineteenth. It allows them to forget a few holes and the only way they'll find water is to order it.

I bought my golf clubs at one of those discount warehouse stores where everything is sold in bulk. I like them, except I don't know what to do with the other three sets.

Our skills will vary as we learn the game of golf. Things can change a great deal in fifty years.

The swing is one of the easiest skills to learn in golf. I learn a new one every time I hit a golf ball.

"My wife said that if I really cared about her, I would give up at least one of the activities that I enjoy," one husband said to another.

"So, which activity did you decide to give up?" the other husband asked. "Golf?"

"No," the first husband replied. "Fortunately for me, I don't enjoy golf. However, I do enjoy painting the house and cleaning up the yard. So I gave those up."

"Tell me about your golf game this morning," one golfer said to another at a party.

"I can't," the other golfer answered.

"Why not?" the first golfer asked.

"Sore ankle," the other golfer replied.

"You couldn't play golf this morning because you had a sore ankle?" the first golfer said.

"I played all right," the other golfer replied. "I'm just not allowed to talk about it at a party because that's where my wife kicks me."

"When would you say you have met your goal, and when would you say you have exceeded your goal?" a golfer was asked.

After some thought, he answered, "I would say I have exceeded my goal when I find my golf ball in the fairway."

"Oh? Then when would you say you have met your goal?"

"When I find my golf ball."

Women and men talk about the same amount on a golf course.

Women talk to each other. Men talk to everything else.

"I had a bad game today," one golfer said to another. "I spent most of the day in the rough, I shot twenty-five over par, I lost a bet on every hole, I can't find my five iron, I . . . ."

"So," the other golfer interrupted, "what was the bad part?"

"I heard that a golfer was so frustrated with his game yesterday," one golfer said to another, "that he threw his clubs into a lake and vowed he'd never play again."

"I know," the other golfer replied. "That was me."

"Golfing runs in the family," one golfer said to another.

"Really?" the other golfer replied. "On your side or your wife's side?"

Before a golfer sliced his ball into a lake, all of the club fit into his bag. After his shot, only part of the club fit into his bag - the part before the right angle.

"I'm thinking about writing a book on how to maintain a perfect golf swing."

"Oh, a fantasy."

A good golf swing is a matter of timing. We have to time our swing so that the club head goes through the ball just a moment before, or just a moment after, we actually do it.

A golf pro was asked, "How often do you hit a golf ball into a lake?"

He answered, "If it's really deep with steep sides, I only hit it in once."

My husband's golf games are getting better. I used to fall asleep after he said, "Let me tell you about the great round I played today . . . ." Now I fall asleep after he says, "Let me tell you . . . ."

An old timer was introducing a younger golfer to the game.

"Golf is really quite easy once you get the hang of it," he said.

"Is that so?" the younger golfer replied. "And how long have you been golfing?"

"Oh, I'd say about thirty-five years," the old timer replied.

"And how long did it take you to get the hang of it?" the younger golfer asked.

"Don't know yet," the old timer answered. "I've only been golfing for thirty-five years."

Timing is crucial in the golf swing. We have to time our swing so that the group ahead is out of range.

"Sometimes I think you love golf more than you love me," a wife complained.

"Only when I'm playing well," her husband answered.

First wife: "I finally stopped my husband from correcting my swing by changing where I tee up my ball."
Second wife: "Really? Where do you tee up your ball now?"
First wife: "In another foursome."

"Is this green difficult to hit?" one golfer asked another.

"It can't be too difficult," the other golfer replied. "The foursome on that other fairway have hit it twice."

"Which club should I use for this shot?" a wife asked her husband.

"Your three wood," he suggested.

After slicing her ball into a lake, she asked again, "Which club should I use for this shot?"

"Your three wood," he suggested.

"That's what you told me last time," she said, "and look what happened."

In spite of the occasional joke about golfers forgetting to include strokes on their score card, we don't believe that many do. It's just that after hitting two shots into a lake, three more to get out of a rough, another five to get out of a sand trap, and then four putting, it's easy to forget a few.

A golfer thought he had a five on a hole, then he thought he had a four, then he thought he had a three. On further thought, he believed it was a four. Not being sure, the golfer who was keeping score gave him a sixteen.

A wife finally admitted that her husband could hit a golf ball farther than she could.

"On our first drives of the day," she said, "my ball went only two hundred yards, while my husband's ball went three hundred and fifty yards . . . and also cleared four houses."

"I went golfing this morning, and I met this gentleman who wasn't in a very good mood, and I said to him, every once in a while we have to stop and smell the roses."

"And what did he say?"

"Get out of my flower bed."

I'm saving a fortune on golf. I can't get a tee time. I'm telling you, I'm saving a fortune.

Last Saturday I played the best round of golf I ever had, and I thought that at last the golfing gods were smiling down on me.

This Saturday I discovered they were just having a bit of fun with me.

* * * * * * *

acadiascale.com

**Acadia Scale Press books
may be purchased at
amazon.com
barnes&noble.com
Barnes & Noble Book Stores
Borders Book Stores
borders.com
and other book and gift stores.**

**Most stores will be happy to order books
if they do not have a copy in stock.
Stores may order through
INGRAM BOOK COMPANY
BAKER & TAYLOR BOOKS
and other book distributors.**

www.ingramcontent.com/pod-product-compliance
Lightning Source LLC
Chambersburg PA
CBHW070842100426
42813CB00003B/714